DEDICATION

To all the members of the body of Christ at the Greenforest Community Baptist Church who have been led by God through spiritual church growth principles to surrender and commit themselves to "Breaking the Huddle" by participation in person-to-person evangelism and becoming "telling witnesses."

To my lovely, devoted wife, Sadie, who has been the leading witness, promoter, public relations person, and huddle breaker for our ministry during its entire life span.

To my three smart, powerful, handsome sons, who have all confessed Jesus Christ as their personal Lord and Savior and who I pray will grow even stronger in the Lord.

ACKNOWLEDGEMENTS

First, as always, I would like to give praise and acknowledge the presence of God and the inspiration of the Holy Spirit, without whom nothing in this book would have been written.

To Olivia M. Cloud and Guardian Angel Communication Services for technical formatting assistance, as well as for preparation of the final manuscript, I extend words of grateful acknowledgement.

Also, I would like to acknowledge Susan Smith for her editorial assistance and the preparation of the study guides.

Finally, I want to acknowledge the work of Gillespie Graphics for their creativity in designing the book cover.

TABLE
of
CONTENTS

PROLOGUE
Breaking the Huddle Through Divine Persuasion 11

CHAPTER ONE
Breaking the Huddle 17
Study Guide 28

CHAPTER TWO
Faithful Over a Few Things 31
Study Guide 39

CHAPTER THREE
Love the Essential Principle 43
Study Guide 54

CHAPTER FOUR
The Importance of Relationships 57
Study Guide 68

CHAPTER FIVE
Evangelize in Deep Water 71
Study Guide 82

CHAPTER SIX

Just Can't Keep It to Myself 85

Study Guide 95

CHAPTER SEVEN

Boldly Stepping Over the Line 99

Study Guide 112

CHAPTER EIGHT

Go a Little Further and Step a Little Higher 115

Study Guide 130

CHAPTER NINE

Be Careful How You Build Your Ministry 133

Study Guide 142

CHAPTER TEN

A Prepared Soil for a Divine Harvest 145

Study Guide 157

CHAPTER ELEVEN

Lift Up Your Eyes and Utilize the Keys to the Harvest.. 161

Study Guide 175

CHAPTER TWELVE

Don't Let the Harvest Pass You By 179

Study Guide 191

EPILOGUE

Time Is Winding Down 195

BIBLIOGRAPHY 198

FOREWORD

Dr. George McCalep's book, *Breaking the Huddle*, is a compilation of messages that have been a part of his lecture series on church growth at both the eighty-second and eighty-third annual gatherings of the renowned Hampton Ministers' Conference.

As president of the Hampton Ministers' Conference, I am privileged to know the results of the formal evaluation of our lectures, as well as informal feedback from the 8,000 registered participants. The evaluations and feedback on Dr. McCalep's lecture series have overwhelmingly been rated as "outstanding" and "excellent." One sentence taken from the descriptive feedback is, "He helped me ..." Over and over we have heard this comment relative to Dr. McCalep's messages… "He helped me."

If a football team is to be successful, it must break the huddle and run the play. Likewise, the church must do the same. Dr. McCalep asserts that the problem with the local church is that it never (or very seldom) breaks the huddle. The analogy is a strong creative illustration of what the church must do if she is to be obedient to God's purpose.

All twelve messages in this book focus toward the goal line of effective outreach. I believe that if pastors and congregations would preach, teach and study these persuasive, Scripture-based messages, they will be led into obedience, carrying out the purposes of the Church as mandated by God. It is without hesitation that I highly recommend this book to pastors, leaders and members of all denominations and churches who are concerned with doing His will.

Dr. McCalep's twelve messages in *Breaking the Huddle* are, true to his style, helping messages. They are designed to move congregations from simply being hearers of the Word to indeed being doers of the Word. This book is about implementing the task of evangelism.

The study sections at the end of each message give the book added useability. Not only can this book be read for enjoyment and information, it can be studied on church leadership retreats and in general Bible study classes.

In *Breaking the Huddle*, Dr. McCalep draws from his experiences as a former athlete to present a creative analogy between the church and a football team trying to carry out a plan to win the game.

Dr. Jesse Battle, Jr., president
Hampton Minister's Conference

PROLOGUE

Breaking the Huddle Through Divine Persuasion

WOE TO THEM
THAT
ARE AT EASE
IN ZION…

INTRODUCTION

Breaking the Huddle is a compilation of messages designed to move the church from its comfort zone and into action. As the Bible says in Amos 6:1, "Woe to them that are at ease in Zion…"

These messages have been delivered across the United States at church growth conferences and Baptist evangelistic rallies and referenced in lectures at the eighty-second and eighty-third annual gatherings of the renowned Hampton Ministers' Conference.

They have been prepared to further illuminate the seven critical church growth principles put forth in one of my previous works, *Faithful Over a Few Things* (Orman Press, 1996). Designed as a companion piece to that work, *Breaking the Huddle* is to be read by congregations, church members and church leaders. This book will also serve as a guide for ministers to develop messages based on critical church growth principles.

Both these works can be effectively synergized by weaving the seven principles from *Faithful Over a Few Things* into these messages according to an individual congregation's current needs and obstacles to church growth.

MESSAGES, NOT SERMONS

This is a book of "messages," as opposed to "sermons." Early in my pastorate, I determined that I should stop preaching "sermons," and start delivering "messages." I am sure that a well-planned sermon can be just as complete as any message; the difference in terminology may be a matter of mere semantics. In my mind, however, sermons are often entertaining but may or may not call for the unbeliever or the church member to come to a point of decision. Sermons are often more edifying than evangelistic. Usually, the only evangelistic emphasis in sermons comes at the end when the invitation is given, directed toward nonbelievers.

> SERMONS CAN BE BIBLICAL AND YET FAIL TO CONNECT TO THE CONTEMPORARY NEEDS OF THE PEOPLE.

Sermons can be biblical and yet fail to connect to the contemporary needs of the people. Sermons sometimes inspire and yet don't inform. At other times they inform and don't inspire.

MOVING FROM POINT 'A' TO POINT 'B'

Since the majority of people to whom we preach are already believers, messages are always designed to move people, primarily believers, from point 'A' to point 'B'. Messages are prophetic. Prophetic preaching always calls people back to God. Messages call for believers (especially church members) to make a decision. Each time a believer comes to church, he or she should be challenged to be a better person after hearing the message. When a message inspires the hearers to make a decision to move from point 'A' to point 'B', they will then be in a position to do what I call, "break the huddle." What does it mean to break the huddle?

> EACH TIME A BELIEVER COMES TO CHURCH, HE OR SHE SHOULD BE CHALLENGED TO BE A BETTER PERSON AFTER HEARING THE MESSAGE.

BREAKING THE HUDDLE

"Breaking the huddle" refers to people in the church, individually and collectively, leaving the comfort zone of rhetoric to become doers of the Word and not hearers only. Imagine the church as a football team that (except when behind and time is running out) huddles between plays to discuss and plan the next play. After a brief instructional encounter with the team, the leader breaks the huddle and runs the play.

> THE PROBLEM IS THAT THE CHURCH SELDOM BREAKS THE HUDDLE.

We huddle together in the church to receive inspiration to go into the community to carry out the established mission of Christ. The problem is that the church seldom breaks the huddle. The huddle often moves, but hardly ever breaks. The church huddle moves from the church to the parking lot, but never fully breaks. It may move from one church to another as we go visiting on Sunday after-

PREACHING IS DIVINE PERSUASION. BREAKING THE HUDDLE IS ABOUT DIVINE PERSUASION DESIGNED FOR A DIVINE PURPOSE.

noon. The church huddle moves from one holy place to another holy place, but hardly ever to the marketplace!

We cannot effectively witness to a dying, lost world in the huddle – it is time to break out of it. Two lines of distinction exist in this illustration: (1) the line of scrimmage; and (2) the goal line. In football, the scrimmage line is the beginning point. The object of the game is to advance beyond the line of scrimmage to the second line, which is the goal line or the desired place. Once you come in contact with the goal line, having the ball in your possession, a score results.

In church growth, the scrimmage line is where your church is now. You may be mid-field, or you may have your back against the opponent's goal line. The idea is to move your church from the scrimmage line where you are now to the goal line and join God in His agenda. To accomplish this task, you must first break the huddle. Nothing happens until you do this. You cannot score touchdowns in the huddle. You cannot kick field goals from the huddle. You cannot put points on the scoreboard from the huddle.

BREAKING THE HUDDLE REQUIRES A WILLINGNESS ON THE PART OF PLAYERS TO MOVE INTO ACTION.

Breaking the huddle requires a willingness on the part of players to move into action. These twelve messages are designed to inspire and encourage today's congregations to break the huddle and share not only the love of Jesus, but also their love for Jesus.

Messages always deal with contemporary issues. Messages provide a prophetic word from God pertaining to everyday living. These messages will help both the pastor and congregation implement the seven critical church growth principles with supportive sermonic persuasion.

> PREACHING IS DIVINE PERSUASION. BREAKING THE HUDDLE IS ABOUT DIVINE PERSUASION DESIGNED FOR A DIVINE PURPOSE.

This book is intended to prepare and spiritually grow the average church member to a higher level of understanding and receptiveness to effective church growth. It is quite suitable for church-wide use, containing questions for interactive Bible study at the end of each message.

PREACHING DIVINE PERSUASION

Time is winding down! We are losing a dying world to the wicked one and his team of angels. It's time to break the huddle! We need to play the game of evangelism effectively before the great scoreboard in heaven is turned off. We must seek and save.

It has been said that preaching is divine persuasion. *Breaking the Huddle* is about divine persuasion designed for a divine purpose. The divine purpose is to persuade the Church to leave the holy place and go to the marketplace. The sacred position of the pulpit must be utilized as a station where transforming prophecy is pronounced.

If the Church is to move from her comfort zone of simply gathering on Sunday morning, we must use Sunday morning "prime time" to get the message of breaking the huddle into the hearts of the people. Preach and teach breaking the huddle! Ask the Lord to help you make these messages speak to you and your church with the power of divine persuasion.

BREAKING THE HUDDLE

Breaking the Huddle
Matthew 17:1-8

> TO HUDDLE UP
> IS TO BEHAVE
> AS IF WE
> HAVE A SECRET.

THE CHURCH IS IN A HUDDLE

The word "huddle," in a generic sense, means to gather together or to get close to one another. It means to come closer together, as though no one outside the huddle should know what's going on in the huddle. To huddle up is to behave as if we have a secret.

Often after worship on Sunday, I see people huddled up in the parking lot. When I walk by the huddle, the huddle gets tighter. You can't hear what they're saying because they're right up on each other. I say to them, "I don't know what you're talking about but I know what you're not talking about. You're not talking about sports. You're not talking about politics. You're not talking about foreign or domestic affairs, or world politics, and you are not talking about Jesus."

Many Americans are avid football fans. Even if you are not a player, a fan or a spectator, for approximately one-third of the year our nation is literally inundated by football via all forms of media, especially television. Since football is so common, I think most people can identify with the concept of a huddle. After each play, the football team huddles up. They draw together closely, and the quarterback calls a predesignated play. He calls a play number like "122," and says "long pass" or "go down the left and cut across." After they finish huddling, they usually clap their hands, break the huddle and then go out to run the game plan.

IT'S TIME FOR THOSE IN THE HOLY PLACE TO GO TO THE MARKETPLACE.

The Lord showed me in a vision that *the Church is in a huddle.* We huddle every Sunday morning in worship and Bible classes. When we leave church on Sunday, however, we just continue to huddle. We huddle again on Monday. We huddle on Tuesday; we huddle on Wednesday; we huddle on Thursday Friday, and Saturday. Then we come back Sunday and get in another big huddle.

It's time for the Church to break the huddle. It's harvest time! It's time for those in the holy place to go to the marketplace. It's time to take a piece of the rock to the pieces of (broken) people. It's time for us to break the huddle and execute God's game plan.

God gave us the game plan in Christ. The game plan is to let somebody know what the Lord has done for you. The game plan is to save a dying, lost, unregenerated, unchurched world.

JESUS CHRIST HAS THE GAME PLAN

I want to propose to you that the game plan came in Christ. Christ's purpose was to save us from our sins and reconcile us back to the Father. Christ's game plan should be our game plan, but we need to break the huddle and run the plays! We cannot implement the game plan as long as we stay huddled up with fellow church members and Christians. In football, you cannot score a touchdown or field goal as long as the team remains in the huddle. Likewise, we cannot fulfill God's game plan as long as we are in the huddle. It is time for the Church to break the huddle! We've got the plan, and we know that the plan is God's.

God sent Christ to lay down His life for us as the ultimate living sacrifice to pay the price of our sin. The game plan deals with our response to what God has already done in Christ and our responsibility to share it with every person in this lost and dying world.

> THE GAME PLAN DEALS WITH OUR RESPONSE TO WHAT GOD HAS ALREADY DONE IN CHRIST, AND TO SHARE IT WITH EVERY PERSON IN THIS LOST AND DYING WORLD.

A BIBLICAL EXAMPLE OF BREAKING THE HUDDLE

In Matthew 17:1-8, Jesus gives us a lesson on the necessity of breaking the huddle. He teaches us how we are strengthened by the glory we can experience during mountaintop experiences in worship – but the call is to go to the valley! For six days Jesus and three of His disciples had been in intense training in discipleship and evangelism. On the seventh day, the day of completion, Jesus thought he would give them one more lesson. He took Peter, James and John to the mountaintop with him. When they got there, the Bible says that He was transfigured before them, shown in all His glory. "His face did shine as the sun, and his raiment was white as light."

The three disciples Peter, James, and John looked around and Peter probably said something like, "Jesus, let us stay here. This

> SOME OF US HAVE GOTTEN SO SPIRITUAL AND HOLY THAT WE'RE SPIRITUALLY FAT.

is too good. This is as close to glory as we have ever been. Let us build you a huddle; let us tabernacle here for a while. Let us build a residence for you."

Peter, James and John wanted to stay, build a tabernacle, and reside there. "We'll build a huddle for Moses, one for Elijah, and one for you, Lord. Let's just all huddle here on the mountaintop." But then a voice came from heaven saying: "Verily, this is my beloved son in whom I am well pleased – hear ye Him." They bowed down in awe and worshiped him. But Jesus came, touched them on the shoulders and said: "Arise. Don't be afraid." We have got work to do. It is time to break the huddle. It is time to go to the valley.

THE PROBLEM

The problem with breaking the huddle is that some of us church people are selfish. I call it, "saint selfishness." It's a spiritual (disease) syndrome. Some of us have gotten so spiritual and holy that we're spiritually fat. We're so spiritually fat and out of shape that we can't run and tell anyone

> THE CHURCH IS HAPPY IN JESUS, BUT ISN'T TELLING ANYONE ABOUT JESUS!

about Jesus! We can buy books, go to conferences, get in our cars and play our spiritual tapes, yet we don't want to get out of our cars and tell anyone about Jesus.

If you're old enough to remember Fats Domino, he sang a song about a happy family: Molly and me, and the baby makes three ... We're happy in our blue heaven. It describes very well the spiritual syndrome of today's church. The Church is happy in Jesus, but isn't telling anyone about Jesus! We need to break the huddle!

TELLING ABOUT EVERYTHING EXCEPT JESUS

We don't want to tell anyone about Jesus. Yet when we go see a good movie, we want to tell everybody! We get excited, and can hardly wait to get back home to tell our friends to go see it.

During the O.J. Simpson trial, those who watched the trial would even tell other people what kind of tie defense attorney Johnny Cochran had on or what prosecutor Marcia Clark was wearing that day. I know this is true because several times people approached me and let me know I was wearing a "Johnnie Cochran" tie! When have you been that excited to tell someone about Jesus? Think about this. Jesus has saved us from the eternity of a hot, burning hell, yet we would rather tell someone about the Atlanta Falcons or the the NFL or Johnny Cochran's tie than to tell them about Jesus. The others haven't done anything for us, whereas Jesus saved our souls!

It is interesting that Moses and Elias were present on the mountaintop during the transfiguration along with the disciples. No one had found Moses' body, but he was supposed to be dead. The Bible tells us that Elias had gone on to heaven, bypassing death in a chariot of fire. That lets us know one thing that we need to remember. We'll have some knowledge of each other in heaven or hell because we'll retain some identifiable characteristics. We'll know our friends in heaven or hell! Friends don't let friends miss out on heaven! Friends don't let friends burst hell wide open!

What can believers do to avoid "saint selfishness" or being spiritually fat?

JESUS DIDN'T
SPEND MUCH
TIME IN
THE TEMPLE

FOCUS ON JESUS

The first thing we need to learn in order to avoid becoming spiritually fat is that when there is a focus on Jesus and Jesus alone, the huddle will be broken. Matthew 17:8 says, "And when they had lifted up their eyes, they saw no man save Jesus alone." When we keep our eyes on Jesus, we won't have time to stay in the huddle because Jesus is not in the huddle. Jesus didn't spend much time in the temple. Check the Bible out on this! Jesus did most of His work elsewhere, not inside the walls of the religious institution. If we have our eyes on Jesus and we're following Him, we won't be in the huddle either.

When Jesus healed blind Bartimaeus, He wasn't in the huddle. When He healed the demoniac, He wasn't in a huddle. When He fed over 5,000 people with a little boy's lunch, He wasn't in the huddle. When He turned water into wine, He wasn't in the huddle. Jesus performed very few miracles in the church and did very little healing in the church. Acknowledging this truth causes me to have some problems with some of my "co-pastors" who are definitely in a huddle.

It occurred to me that some people I've never met co-pastor with me at the church that God called me to pastor. Who are they? They are the preachers that church members watch on television. Whether I like it or not, I have some co-pastors among the group of televangelists and religious personalities – and I have problems with some of them, particularly the "faith healers."

I believe in healing because I have personally experienced a physical healing from God. However, I don't understand why, when God has given someone the gift of healing, that person can't or doesn't go to the hospital and heal someone there? Why does healing have to happen in the church? If God has given me the gift of healing, I need to go to the hospitals and lay hands on sick people. Think about that.

Some of us will huddle with faith healers from all over the country, spending lots of money, buying airline tickets, and buying tapes to get a blessing. We play their tapes, get our blessing, and yet we won't bless anyone else by sharing what we've heard! When we do this, our spiritual eyes may be focused on many things, but they aren't focused on Jesus. If we keep Jesus in focus, we won't be able to stay in the huddle.

GIVE JESUS A STRONG LIFT

Jesus' purpose was to seek and save lost people. If we are to do His work with Him, we must break the huddle and follow Jesus, keeping Him in the forefront. We must lift up high the name of Jesus.

The Million Man March in 1995 consisted of one million Black men marching on Washington, D.C. with an expressed purpose of focusing the nation's attention on the importance of the Black male to the Black family. Although it was an incredible event, I had a major concern about it. Jesus was not leading that tremendous outpouring, and He was not lifted up in their efforts. The March was an attempt to treat the symptom and not the disease causing the symptom. The real cause of all the violence and the injustice in this country is that we have not learned and internalized that Jesus is the answer to all of our problems. While many churches are lifting Jesus up, it's only a "weak lift."

What do I mean by a "weak lift?" Have you ever gone to a health club to work out and used those five-pound plastic bar

> IF WE GIVE HIM
> A STRONG LIFT
> BY BREAKING OUT
> OF OUR HUDDLE,
> MEN AND WOMEN
> WILL COME RUNNING
> UNTO HIM.

bells in step aerobics? You're not really doing a lot of lifting when you use those little weights during exercise. It doesn't take much out of you to lift them!

In the real weight room, however, the strong men and women are truly pumping iron! They're working hard, and it takes all they have to do it. When you go to the real weight room, you've got to bend your knees and go all the way down to get the barbell. When you get a good hold on it, you have to jerk it up to lift it up.

Saints, we need to bend our knees, go down all the way, get a good hold on Jesus, and give Him a strong lift up high until He speaks from eternity. Jesus told us that if He is lifted up, He will draw all people unto Himself. If we give Him a strong lift by breaking out of our huddle, men and women will come running unto Him.

MOUNTAINTOP EXPERIENCES HAVE A PURPOSE

We need to learn that God doesn't give us mountaintop experiences for no reason. Spiritual renewal always has a purpose. God took Peter, James and John up on the mountaintop for a reason. He let Peter, James and John see Jesus transfigured before them to experience a foretaste of glory divine, but it wasn't just for that alone! It was the seventh day of their training.

In the Bible, seven is a number representing completeness. They had experienced six days of good training, but they needed a little more to complete their lesson. God had prepared them, but now He needed to strengthen them for the crucifixion. He needed to strengthen them for the resurrection. He needed to prepare them to be able to live a resurrected life as disciples of a risen Savior. When we have a mountaintop experience, it has a purpose. God doesn't bring us to the mountaintop just to leave us there.

> WHEN WE HAVE A MOUNTAINTOP EXPERIENCE, IT HAS A PURPOSE. GOD DOESN'T BRING US TO THE MOUNTAINTOP JUST TO LEAVE US THERE.

The mountaintop is a glorious experience. They were happy on the mountaintop! They felt true joy on the mountaintop! They knew Jesus was there with them on the mountaintop! They wanted to stay in that huddle on the mountaintop forever, but Jesus directed them to, "Break the huddle!"

Sometimes when we come to church, God gives us mountaintop experiences. Sometimes I get so happy in church I just can't help myself!

We rejoice on the mountaintop! We praise God on the mountaintop! We get spiritual feelings of euphoria on the mountaintop! Sometimes I feel I could stay at church all day! Sometimes it is really hard to go back down to the valley.

I love to praise the Lord! I love to worship the Lord! I love to be in His presence on the mountaintop! Yet God lets us know we have to, Break the huddle! Go to the valley! God says, "I didn't bring you up here just for yourself. I brought you up here to strengthen you, to fill you up, to service you."

One of my favorite sayings is, "It is not how high you jump on Sunday, but which way you land, and where you go when you hit the ground." As followers of Christ, it is our responsi-

> GOD THE
> HOLY GHOST
> BROKE THE HUDDLE
> WHEN HE LEFT
> THE COMFORT OF
> HIS THRONE ON THE
> DAY OF PENTECOST
> TO DWELL IN THE
> HEARTS OF THE SAINTS.

bility to go to the valley and to the marketplace. We must go forth and break the huddle!

THEY BROKE THE HUDDLE IN THE BIBLE

Abraham broke the huddle when he went and looked for a city. Nehemiah broke the huddle when he left his cup-bearing position to go back to Jerusalem to build up the torn down walls and the burning gates. Peter and Andrew broke the huddle when they put down their fishing poles and became fishers of men. Paul and Barnabas broke the huddle when they left Antioch and began preaching the Gospel in Asia and Europe.

God the Father, God the Son and God the Holy Ghost broke the huddle! God the Father broke the huddle when He made humankind in His own image. God the Son broke the huddle when He thought it was not robbery, so mindful of humanity, that He robed himself in flesh and stepped down out of eternity into time to save a sin-sick world – to minister, bleed and die for all of humanity. God the Holy Ghost broke the huddle when He left the comfort of His throne on the Day of Pentecost to dwell in the hearts of the saints.

YOU NEED TO BREAK THE HUDDLE

You need to break the huddle yourself! You may be huddling in yourself, huddling in your children, huddling in your job, huddling at your church, huddling in your pride, huddling in doing your own thing. God says, "Break the huddle."

Will you dare to do the hard work it takes to break out of the comfort zones of rhetoric? Will you break out of the comfort of the five-pound plastic barbell that, at best, gives Him a weak lift? God is ready to show you the huddle you're in if you're ready to see it. He is ready to give you the mountaintop experiences that will strengthen you for the valley.

> HE IS READY TO GIVE YOU THE MOUNTAINTOP EXPERIENCES THAT WILL STRENGTHEN YOU FOR THE VALLEY.

Break the huddle and go to the valley. Go into the real weight room, where the strong men and women can be found ready to execute the next play in God's game plan for growing the church!

CHAPTER ONE
STUDY GUIDE

1. Give the definition of a huddle.

2. Name three kinds of church huddles people like to stay in.

3. What is God's game plan? What position are you playing in this game?

4. Who was in the huddle that occurred in Matthew 17:1-8?

5. Being in a huddle can be a good thing. Give two reasons God called the disciples into a huddle on the mountaintop in Matthew 17:1-8.

6. How did the disciples propose to stay in the huddle with Jesus? Why did they want to stay in the huddle?

7. What was Jesus' answer to the disciple's proposal to stay in the huddle? Why did He respond that way?

8. Explain how Jesus' ministry was an example of how one consistently breaks the huddle.

9. What is "saint selfishness"? How have you been a selfish saint?

10. Fill in the blanks:

    Friends don't let _____ miss _____.

    Friends don't let friends _____ _____ _____ open.

For Deeper Study

1. Read Genesis chapters twelve and thirteen. Why did Abram break the huddle? What did he sacrifice?

2. Read Nehemiah chapters one and two. Describe how Nehemiah broke the huddle. Why did he want to do it?

HUDDLE GROUP DISCUSSION

1. This message describes the problems that occur when the church gets in a huddle and stays there. Discuss this problem from your own perspective in ministry.

2. What are the most significant factors that cause individual ministries or the church as a whole to stay huddled up?

3. How can church leaders help facilitate breaking the huddle in ministry?

BREAK THE HUDDLE!

What comfort zone ministry huddle have you stayed in for too long? What will you do to break out of this huddle so that you can run another play in God's game plan?

Breaking the Huddle 2

Faithful Over a Few Things
Matthew 25:14-29

> I SAW MYSELF AS A
> MAN IN A CARNIVAL,
> THE MAN WHO TRIES
> TO KEEP SPINNING
> SAUCERS ON A POLE.

SPINNING THE SAUCERS OF MINISTRY

God has blessed us in such miraculous ways at Greenforest that it has caused people from all over the country to want to know our story. People both Black and White have taken notice of our church and our ministries and have invited me to come tell our story, alongside the great church leaders of this country. They all want to know how did we do it? Over and over, I keep saying that *we* didn't do it – God did it. To *God* be the glory!

However, it isn't enough to say to some people that God did it. They want to know how did God do it? How did God work through you to do it? So I encapsulated the seven essential principles of church growth that have been effective for us over the past eighteen years in a book entitled *Faithful Over A Few Things* (Orman Press, 1996). The inspiration for that book came when I saw myself as a man in a carnival, the man who tries to keep spinning saucers on a pole. My carnival act began by getting one saucer spinning; then moving on to get the next saucer spinning, then to the next, and the next, etc. There was a limitation, however, on how many saucers I could keep spinning at one time! Sooner or later, the first saucer would begin to wobble and I would have to run back to get it spinning again. If I tried to keep too many spinning at once, all the saucers would fall to the floor because I couldn't keep up!

The analogy seemed to fit me because I saw myself doing ministry the same way. First I would get the Sunday School saucer spinning. Then I would get the evangelism saucer spinning and, as soon as it was looking good, I would move on to the worship service saucer; then the stewardship saucer, etc.... Sooner or later, the Sunday School saucer would begin to wobble, and I would run back to get it going again. Then others would begin to wobble. I found myself constantly running from saucer to saucer in an exhausting attempt to keep them all spinning at once. I got behind, and they all began to wobble and fell to the ground at the same time. Incredibly frustrated, I just let them lay there for a while. I must honestly confess, I took a paid vacation mentally and didn't tell anyone. I just let them lay there because I was frustrated, tired and I didn't know what more to do. Then the Lord picked me up and began to teach me that *I can't do everything,* which is a message for all of us. We can't do everything, but we can do a few things well. I learned to put first things first, to be time-focused. To illustrate this point, journey with me through Matthew 25:14-29.

> WE CAN'T DO EVERYTHING, BUT WE CAN DO A FEW THINGS WELL.

FAITHFUL CHURCH-SITTING

In this well-known parable of the talents, Jesus said that a certain man took a journey. This certain man was the Lord. Before He went on His journey, He called His servants to do some, "creation-sitting," or what we might call today "church-sitting." Understand that if you are asked to sit with something, you do not own it. Also, you should keep it as nice as you found it, and, hopefully, improve its condition while it is in your care to demonstrate that you are a worthy "sitter."

HE CALLED HIS SERVANTS TO DO SOME, "CREATION-SITTING," OR WHAT WE MIGHT CALL TODAY "CHURCH-SITTING."

Before the Lord left on His journey, He blessed each of His servant creation-sitters with some talents to care for in His absence. To one servant He gave five talents; to another He gave two; and to another He gave one. He gave to each one according to their individual abilities. In other words, He gave them talents according to what He knew to be their ability to manage them. Because He gave each one a commensurate number of talents, it was reasonable for Him to expect that each servant would be able to do well with his "creation-sitting" duty.

The one who had five talents worked hard to use and develop them, as did the one who had been given two. The "creation-sitter" who had been given one talent dug a hole and hid his talent in the earth for safe-keeping instead of using it. When the Lord came back, He was pleased with the two servants who had been busy sitting with His creation, working to improve and develop their talents while He was away. In Matthew 25:21, He praised each: "Well done thou good and faithful servant; thou has been faithful over a few things, I will make thee ruler over many things: enter thou into the joy of thy lord." They had done a good job managing their responsibilities while he was away.

The servant who had buried his talent began making excuses. I imagine the conversation went something like this: "Lord, I have Your one talent here. I know You are a hard man. I mean, I saw how Michelangelo painted Your picture in the Sistine Chapel. You were looking mean, Lord. I didn't read the Bible about your grace and mercy. I just accepted Michelangelo's artistic expression of You. I was afraid of failing. I was afraid of disappointing You. I hid my talent, Lord. I knew you wouldn't want us putting money in a building campaign when we still have room in this building. Lord, I knew You didn't want us spending money on Sunday School materials when You gave us the Bible. I knew You didn't want us spending money on training because the Holy Spirit leads us. Lord, I knew You didn't want us concerned with employment, housing for the elderly, credit unions or economic empowerment in the church when all the power already belongs to us. So Lord, I hid Your money. I hid your talent You gave me. I took no risk. I refused to be on the cutting edge of ministry because I might fail!"

> WHERE HAVE
> YOU HIDDEN
> YOUR GIFT(S) OR
> SPIRITUAL TALENT(S)?

The Lord was not pleased with this servant's lack of faith and initiative. This one had done nothing as a creation-sitter while the Master was away. He had completely failed because he had avoided all risk based on a fear of failure. He had not appreciated his blessing. Instead of trying to spin his saucer, he buried it to be certain it wouldn't fall off the pole and break. In Matthew 25:26-29, the Lord told this servant: "...Thou wicked and slothful servant, thou knewest that I reap where I sowed not, and gather where I have not strawed: Thou oughtest therefore to have put my money to the exchangers and then at my coming I should have received mine own with usury. Take therefore the talent from him, and give it unto him which hath ten talents. For unto every one that hath shall be given, and he shall have abundance: but

> THAT DORMANT POWER NEEDS TO BE RELEASED THROUGH IDENTIFYING AND UTILIZING OUR SPIRITUAL GIFTS, WHICH ARE THE TALENTS HE HAS GIVEN TO US.

from him that hath not shall be taken away even that which he hath." How does this parable apply to us today? Where have you hidden your gift(s) or spiritual talent(s)?

RELEASING DORMANT POWER

We have a problem with hiding our gifts or talents, too! We (the Church) are not using all that God has given us. That dormant power needs to be released through identifying and utilizing our spiritual gifts, which are the talents He has given to us. Too many church members have these gifts hidden under the pews because they like watching other people spin the saucers! Some people have the gift of helping but aren't helping anyone. Some people have the gift of teaching but don't want the responsibility of teaching in the church. Many have the gift of administration but figure that's what the church staff gets paid to do. Some have the gift of leadership but do not want to lead unless they can be the star of the saucer-spinning act. Still others have the gift of evangelism but leave that to the pastor because he is supposed to be the number one soul-winner.

Spiritual Truths

Three spiritual truths can be gleaned from this Scripture passage. First, God does not mind us using His money to establish and implement wholistic ministries to His glory. Many Christians and churches feel that the role of the church should be limited to that which can be defined as spiritual. Therefore, credit unions, academic centers, social employment assistance, training centers, and other ministries that address the needs of the whole person are not the role of the church. God told the one who serves that he should not be afraid to use his talent so that when He returns he would have that which was given to him – and more. God approves of us using His money to help others. The key to the approach lies in the method and motive. It must be done in a godly manner, and it must all be done for His glory.

Second, God is not interested in what we don't have – He wants us to use what He has given us. God is not interested in our excuses. Too many Christians and church leaders make excuses relative to their lack of resources, skills, abilities, and so forth. God is saying the same thing to us that He said to a complaining Moses, "What is that in your hand?" He is saying, "Haven't I given you at least one spiritual gift? Then use what I have given you."

Third, the Scripture teaches us that if we don't use the gifts that God has given us we may lose those gifts. God took the one gift from the unprofitable servant and gave it to the servant that had invested his gifts. If you don't use it you may lose it. God wants us to use and not lose

> WATER YOUR GIFTS BY USING THEM AND GOD WILL GIVE THE INCREASE.

what He has given us. Be faithful in the utilization of the gifts God has given you.

SEVEN CRITICAL PRINCIPLES

The following are seven critical principles of church growth which are described in depth in, *Faithful Over A Few Things* (Orman Press, 1996):

1. Cherish and prioritize relationships
2. Establish a knowledge-based teaching/preaching foundation
3. Initiate change
4. Prioritize expressive praise and pray in faith
5. Orchestrate intentional evangelism and outreach ministries
6. Assure and monitor assimilation
7. Create small groups

I am working as hard as I can to be faithful over these seven principles. If we are to implement these principles effectively, we need to be faithful in developing our gifts. If you have a gift, *use it,* because in using it, your gift will grow and increase. You don't have to have a lot. Water your gifts by using them and God will give the increase. Whatever your talents or gifts may be, God can use them if you let Him.

Your gift might be most valuable in spinning the saucer of cherishing and nurturing relationships. Are you a "people person?" Do you have the gift of mercy? Are you a gifted teacher? If so, please step up and help spin the saucer of establishing a preaching/teaching ministry of the Word. Are you a creator or a visionary who enjoys taking risks and doing things in a new way? Visionaries are always needed to help keep the saucer of ongoing change spinning on the pole. Does expressive praise and praying in faith come easily to you? Do you *love* to praise the Lord? Are you known as a prayer warrior? If so, the church needs your help spinning the praise/prayer saucer because many saints are just too inhibited to step up in those activities. Do you have a testimony? Are you a good communicator? Has Jesus been so good to you that you just can't keep it to yourself? Almost every Christian has been given a gift in this area and you really need to use it because the outreach/evangelism saucer is usually the one that everybody thinks somebody else has covered so it often falls on the ground!

Perhaps you have a different gift. Do you have the gift of administration? Are you good with numbers and processing information? Monitoring and evaluating the assimilation of new members is a very important saucer that many churches don't even bother to spin. That saucer is too often not even in the act yet! If it is spinning at your church, I am sure your help is needed.

Finally, do you have the gift of facilitating relationship-building among other people? Are you a good organizer with an interest in the details that make the big picture work? If so, you should use your gifts to spin the saucer of creating the small groups that contribute so much to the overall growth of every church.

Get in the Act

We can't do everything, but we all can do a few things well with the gifts we've been given according to our abilities as individuals. Church growth isn't a spectator sport. Although God is pleased to see you in the pew on Sunday, what He really wants is for you to get up and get in the act yourself. Get off the bench! Break the huddle and get into the game!

CHAPTER TWO
STUDY GUIDE

1. What does it mean to be a "creation-sitter" or a "church-sitter?"

2. "Talent" actually means a sum of money in the original Greek manuscript. Why did the Lord give His servants different amounts of talent in Matthew 25:25?

3. How did the servant with five talents and the servant with two talents please the Lord when He returned?

4. What did the Lord say to these two servants in Matthew 25:21 that showed He was pleased with them?

5. The servant with one talent did not please the Lord upon His return. Why?

6. What did the Lord say to the servant with one talent to show His displeasure?

7. In Matthew 25:27, the Lord explains what He had expected all the servants to do with their talents while He was away. Describe this expectation in your own words.

8. Parables use earthly examples to teach us spiritual truths. We have each received spiritual gifts and talents from the Lord to multiply while He is away, rather than a sum of money. What are your gifts or talents?

9. Which of your gifts or talents have you multiplied in ministry work? What helped you set up and spin the saucers in these areas?

10. Which of your gifts and talents need to be used and developed in ministry work? Why have you not yet gotten in the act in these areas?

FOR DEEPER STUDY

1. Read Romans 12:4-8. What is this passage saying about the importance of every member using their gifts?

2. Read 1 Corinthians 12:1-31. How does this passage demonstrate that all gifts are equally important?

HUDDLE GROUP DISCUSSION

This message lists seven critical principles of church growth. Considering your church home, discuss:

(1) Which principle/saucer do you spin best? What makes this one so effective?

(2) Which principle/saucer is wobbling and needs improvement? Why? What needs to be done to get it spinning well again?

(3) Which principle/saucer has fallen on the floor or is not yet in the act? Why? What can you do to get it started spinning?

BREAK THE HUDDLE!

1. What will you do in the next month to multiply one of your gifts in ministry?

2. What will you do in the next month to encourage others to multiply one of their gifts in ministry?

BREAKING THE HUDDLE

Love: The Essential Principle
John 21:15-17

> ...LOVE IS THE PRINCIPLE "MOST LIKELY TO SUCCEED" IN CHURCH GROWTH.

THE MOST ESSENTIAL PRINCIPLE

In *Faithful Over A Few Things*, we focused on seven critical principles for spiritual growth that always lead to church growth. The question may be asked, "Of the seven, which one is the star?" Which one is most essential? Which principle is the most valuable player of the seven? The answer is that Cherishing and Nurturing Relationships wins the "Oscar" for "Essential Principle" in church growth! Jesus said it is the foundation of the two greatest commandments.

In Matthew 22:36, the disciples asked Jesus, "Master, which is the greatest commandment in the law?" Jesus told them, "Thou shalt love the Lord thy God with all thy heart, and with all thy soul, and with all thy mind. This is the first and great commandment. And the second is like unto it, Thou shalt love

> WE'RE SO CAUGHT UP IN MAKING IT IN THE SECULAR WORLD THAT WE NEGLECT THE ESSENTIAL INGREDIENT IN THE CHRISTIAN LIFE.

thy neighbor as thyself. On these two commandments hang all the law and the prophets."

If God summed up the law and the prophets into these two commandments, surely cherishing and nurturing relationships – love – is the principle "Most Likely to Succeed" in church growth. If all we have to do is focus primarily on loving God and each other, why do we have a problem growing the church?

Too Busy to Make a Life

The problem is that we are so busy making a living that we don't have time to make a life. We're so caught up in making it in the secular world that we neglect the essential ingredient in the Christian life. We're sometimes so busy doing church work that we forget what the Church is really designed to do. Sometimes we're so busy working in the church that we don't have time for the church to work in us. As I travel the country speaking at church growth conferences, many pastors have come to me for advice about their situations. I was particularly moved by one pastor who had been so busy doing the work of God that he hadn't had time for God to do any work in Him. I suspect this is the case with many pastors, and certainly other church leaders as well.

The Last Supper – The First Breakfast

We must never lose sight of the fact that the only things that are going to stand when all else is gone are relationships and love. John 21:15-23 illustrates this point very well. The setting of this passage is by the Sea of Tiberius, a beautiful place. Jesus chose this beautiful place to make one of His post-resurrection appearances. Several of the disciples had gone fishing and the beloved disciple, John, recognized Jesus on the shore. Peter got so excited that he couldn't wait until the ship got back. He jumped in the water and swam to shore. Peter was in a backslidden position and out of fellowship because he had denied Jesus before the crucifixion. Still he jumped in the water and began to swim!

> IF YOU'RE IN A BACKSLIDDEN POSITION AND THE LORD GIVES YOU ANOTHER CHANCE, YOU OUGHT TO RUN TO HIM.

This is a lesson for each of us to consider. If you're in a backslidden position and the Lord gives you another chance, you ought to *run* to Him. If somehow you have failed God because you didn't own Him in the workplace, if you know you haven't done all that you should and God gives you another chance, you ought to *jump* in the water and swim back to Him! Peter swam fast toward the Lord for his reordination. After all, God had chosen Peter, but He couldn't use him in a backslidden position. Peter needed restoration so he could go on to do all God had in store for him.

I call this the "First Breakfast" because it is an event similar to the Last Supper. Jesus was in the same posture in which He had been for the Last Supper. At the Last Supper, He washed the disciples' feet. At the First Breakfast, he cooked their meal – still in a role of a servant. At the Last Supper, He broke bread and He passed the cup. At the First Breakfast, He was there with fish and bread. To fully understand the significance of this message, you need to understand whom Peter represents. Peter is every believer. Peter is the best representative character in the Bible for all of humanity.

All of us have denied Christ in our own way. All of us have failed God in some way. We are all Peters! We have all been in a backslidden position. Many of us are there right now. God wants to use all of us just like He used Peter. He took Peter from a backslidden position, filled him with the Holy Spirit and 3,000 got saved when he preached at Pentecost.

> PETER REPRESENTS
> ALL OF US WHO
> HAVE FAILED
> THE LIVING GOD
> IN SOME WAY

He wants to do that with us today. My name and your name is Peter. Think about it. What would you do if someone came on your job with an Uzzi automatic weapon and said, "I'm going to shoot all the Christians." Would you still be a Christian? Say hello, Peter!

THE ESSENTIAL PRINCIPLE – LOVE

Peter represents all of us who have failed the living God in some way. After the disciples had dined with Jesus, He pulled Peter aside and said to him, "Peter, do you love me more than these?" What are "these?" I think Jesus meant, "Do you love me more than these fish? Do you love me more than this bread?" What about you? What is Jesus asking you? "Do you love me more than your job? Do you love me more than your education? Do you love me more than you love your house or your car or other materials things? Do you love me more than you love your money? Do you love me more than you love your wife, your husband, your children or the comfortable huddle that you're in? Do you *agape* me? *Do you love me more than these?"*

Peter said "Yes, Lord, you know I love you." Jesus asked Him again, "Peter, do you love me?" Peter replied, "Yes, Lord." Jesus said to him again, "Feed my lambs. Feed my sheep." In other words, build relationships. Build a biblical community of loving relationships! Jesus says, "Have a relationship with me first, then have a relationship with your neighbor and the mission field." Jesus says, "Have a relationship member-to-member, member-to-pastor, pastor-to-member – build relationships. Feed my sheep!" A third time he asked, "Peter, do you *really* love me?" To fully understand what transpired in this conversation, you need to read it in the Greek manuscript.

> JESUS SAYS, "HAVE A RELATIONSHIP WITH ME FIRST, THEN HAVE A RELATIONSHIP WITH YOUR NEIGHBOR AND THE MISSION FIELD."

The word love can be translated three ways: *eros, phileo,* and *agape.* The first two times Jesus asked, the original manuscript translated love from the root word *"agape,"* or unconditional love. Both times, Peter's answer meant "Yes Lord, I *phileo* (have brotherly love for) you.

The third time Jesus asked, the word love is translated from the Greek word *"phileo."* The third time Jesus asked He meant, "Do you even love me as *phileo?* Can you even love me that much?" Perhaps Jesus was asserting that even having brotherly love calls for one to be a servant. At this, Peter was grieved because he remembered a time not long ago when he stood by a different fire and he had denied knowing the Lord. And he said, "Lord, thou knowest everything." Once again, Jesus said to him, "Feed

... THE ESSENTIAL
PRINCIPLE, LOVE,
ALWAYS FORGIVES
AND GRANTS
ANOTHER CHANCE.

my sheep." In other words, build relationships. Love your neighbor as you love yourself.

We can learn three things about the essential principle, which is love. The first thing we learn from this is that the essential principle, love, always forgives and grants another chance. Do you need to forgive someone and grant him or her another chance? *Agape*, the essential principle, always forgives and grants another chance. Do you need to forgive your spouse, your mother or your father? Maybe you have an earthly father who abandoned you when you were five-years-old and you don't want to forgive him. If you have *agape*, the love of God, you can forgive and grant him another chance. Maybe you have a broken relationship with a child. If you have *agape*, you can forgive that child, and grant another chance.

IN JESUS,
NO FAILURE
IS FINAL. IN JESUS,
YOU CAN ALWAYS
TAKE THE TEST
OVER AGAIN.

In Jesus, no failure is final. In Jesus, you can always take the test over again. I don't know about you, but I'm glad about it. You can't flunk out of His school. With Jesus, you can always re-enroll and try again tomorrow. You need to know that if you have Jesus in your heart, failure doesn't exist because He can't fail. He is always willing to give you another chance. That is really good news to me! With Jesus, there is no such thing as three strikes and you're out for good, because you will always get another turn at bat if you want one!

THE ESSENTIAL QUESTION

The second thing we learn about this essential principle called love is that it is attached to an essential question, "Do you love me?" Do you love Jesus? We ask a lot of questions as Christians and many are important, but others are not. "Who was Noah's grandmother?" is not an important question. Questions about predestination, though, are important, as well as questions about the assurance of eternal salvation. Those are good questions! When we get saved, is there another part to salvation that comes by the filling of the Holy Spirit? That's a good question, but it isn't the essential question, nor the most important question.

> THE SECOND THING WE LEARN ABOUT THIS ESSENTIAL PRINCIPLE CALLED LOVE IS THAT IT IS ATTACHED TO AN ESSENTIAL QUESTION, "DO YOU LOVE ME?"

Jesus asks the essential question: "Do *you* love Me? Do you *love* Me? Do you love *Me?*" The answer to that question is that, if you love Him, no one has to prompt you to go to Bible study because you will want to know more about His Word. If you love Him, you don't want to have "High Attendance Sunday" for Sunday School since every Sunday is high attendance Sunday. If you love Him, no one has to prompt you to tithe because you will want to give Him what belongs to Him. If you love Him, no one has to prompt you to raise your hand to give Him praise, because you'll praise Him anyway. If you love Him, you don't have to be reminded to treat your neighbor right because you know to love your enemy, and even to pray for your enemy because you really love

Him. If you love Him, no one even has to ask you to pick up paper on the church floor because you'll want to keep it clean.

I heard about a popular song in which a girlfriend is singing to her boyfriend. "I just want you to love me like you love your Jeep." What she was saying is "I just want you to love me like you love your Wrangler, like you love your Grand Cherokee Limited ... like you love your Rodeo ... love me like you love your Jeep. You keep your Jeep clean. You change the oil in your Jeep. You don't want anyone else to use, or drive your Jeep. I just want you to demonstrate the same love to me that you have shown to your Jeep."

> JESUS JUST WANTS YOU TO LOVE HIM LIKE YOU LOVE YOUR JEEP ... WHAT IS YOUR JEEP?

The question is, what is your Jeep? Is your job your Jeep? Is your house your Jeep? Is your condo your Jeep? What about your golf clubs, your fishing equipment, your tennis racket or your money? The real question is, "What is your Jeep?" Jesus just wants you to love Him like you love your Jeep.

One night my wife and I were watching television and saw that Ella Fitzgerald, the great jazz singer had died. My wife commented to me, "When I married you, you were into jazz." She was right. I *loved* jazz! I had a great jazz collection. I had MJQ, Diz, Charlie "Yardbird" Parker, Milt Jackson ... I had them all! I loved my jazz collection. We didn't have CD's then, just those big record albums. I had a dust cloth to get the lint out of the grooves and I loved to dust them carefully. I would panic if I heard a scratch – I just couldn't have that! I had to have a diamond-tipped needle because the record wouldn't play just right without one of those.

One day I came home from work, and my then six-month-old son Michael had my jazz collection in the middle of the floor, rolling them against the wall, taking them in his hand having a great time like babies do. I came so close to child abuse that day! I reached down, in anger, to get him. But, praise God, He caught me, and I never bought another record since. I also never went to another jazz club. God took that from me, because I loved my jazz collection ..."more than these."

... THE ESSENTIAL
PRINCIPLE OF LOVE
REQUIRES AN ANSWER
FROM THE
ESSENTIAL PERSON.

Jesus is asking, "Do you love me more that you love these?" What is your "these?" What is your jazz collection? What's your Jeep? Do you love God more than you love "these?" That is the essential question. If loving Jesus were a crime, would there be enough evidence against you to find you guilty? If they subpoenaed your co-workers to come and testify against you, would the prosecution have enough witnesses and evidence to convict you, or would you go free? Think about it.

THE ESSENTIAL PERSON

The third thing we learn is that the essential question about the essential principle of love requires an answer from the essential Person. Who is that essential person? He asked Peter, "Do *you* love Me?" He didn't ask any of the other disciples. He is asking *you*, "Do you love Me?" He isn't asking your neighbor or your friend, your co-worker or your boss. Peter, in verse 21, looks over at John and says to Jesus, "What about that guy?" Isn't that the way we are? "I'm not in this by myself am I, Jesus?" But Jesus is talking to you and you only when He asks the question, *"Do you love Me?"*

>
>
> TOO MANY OF US USE CHURCH HYPOCRISY TO AVOID ANSWERING THE ESSENTIAL QUESTION.

Too many of us use church hypocrisy to avoid answering the essential question. We want to put it off on someone else. Jesus is asking us, but we're saying, "What about that preacher? I heard he's a homosexual."

Jesus responds, "I'm not asking you about that guy. *Do you love Me?*" We reply, "What about that choir member who's shacking up?"

Jesus says, "I didn't ask you about that choir member. Do you love Me?" We keep trying, telling Jesus more irrelevant information, "What about that deacon? I heard he had a baby by one of the sisters in the church!"

Jesus doesn't ask us about any of that! He wants to know, "Do *you* love Me?" Jesus doesn't ask us about the hypocrisy of the church or the hypocrisy of the world. He just wants to ask you and me the essential question. He wants us to answer Him. "Do you love Me? Do you love Me more than these? Do you *agape* Me?"

YES, LORD ... TOTALLY AND COMPLETELY YES

If you have truly been born again, you should be able to answer the question, "Yes, Lord ... totally and completely yes! Without reservation, yes, Lord." Why should you respond "yes?" You should answer yes because God has given you the victory. Love gives the victory! We are more than conquerors through Him who loves us. "I am persuaded that neither death nor life, nor angels, nor principalities, nor powers, nor things present, nor things to come, nor heights, nor depths, nor any other thing or creature can separate us from God's love," (Romans 8:38-39).

Too many of us are like Peter when it comes to our love for Christ. Something can come up and separate our love from God, but *nothing* can separate God's love from us. *Love is the essential element!* When I was a child, I talked like a child, I reasoned like a child. But when I became a man, I put away my jazz collection. When I became a man, I grew up from a spiritual baby and put away childish things.

Love is the essential principle of church growth. In 1 Corinthians 13, the apostle Paul unfolds the quintessential definition of love for believers in Jesus Christ: "If I speak with tongues of men and angels but have not love – I am nothing. If I have the gift of prophecy and know all mysteries, and have faith that can move mountains, but I don't have love – I'm nothing. If I give my possessions to the poor and surrender my body to be burned in flames, but don't have love – I am nothing. Love never fails. For now we see through a glass dimly, but then face-to-face. Now we know in part, but then we shall be known even as we are known. Three things abide – hope, faith and love." All three are good but I don't need faith when I wake up in the arms of the Justifier. I don't need hope when I wake up in the arms of the One I hope to see. When I wake up, I'll be in the arms of He who is *love*, because God is Love and Love is God.

Do you love Him more than you love your Jeep? If you do, you will love God with all your heart and you will gladly love your neighbor as yourself. You will cherish and nurture relationships, which create the foundation upon which all other essential principles of church growth are laid. If you love Him more than "these," you will build a biblical community of loving relationships, modeling and following Christ in everything you do. You won't just talk about loving other people. You will actually do it!

CHAPTER THREE
STUDY GUIDE

1. Which is the *most* essential church growth principle of the seven described in *Faithful Over A Few Things*?

2. What did Jesus say that supports this principle being the most essential role of the church?

3. What are the only things that are going to stand when all else is gone?

4. Why is Peter the best representative character for all of humanity in the Bible?

5. What was Jesus really asking Peter when He said, "Peter, do you love me more than these?"

6. Describe the difference between *phileo* love and *agape.*

7. What was Jesus telling Peter when He said, "Feed my lambs, feed my sheep"?

8. Fill in the blank:

   The essential principle is _____.

   The essential question is _____.

   The essential person is _____.

9. What is your Jeep? Do you love Jesus more than your Jeep? Be honest! God already knows the answer ...

10. Describe how agape love in building relationships will grow the church and make disciples for Jesus Christ.

FOR DEEPER STUDY

1. Read 1 Corinthians 13:1-13, the well known passage about love. On a 1-10 scale, how true is the "love" you give. On a 1-10 scale, how true is the "love" you have received? Be honest!

2. Read I John 4:7-21. Describe what this passage says about the origin and evidence of love in your own words.

HUDDLE GROUP DISCUSSION

1. Would you say cherishing and nurturing relationships is a strength or a weakness in your church's growth? Why?

2. Discuss the statement "We're sometimes so busy working in the church that we don't have time for the church to work in us."

3. How can you find a healthy balance between being active in ministry and having enough time to cherish and nurture relationships in your life?

BREAK THE HUDDLE!

The purest form of *agape* is when you love someone who doesn't deserve it. In Matthew 5:44, Jesus says we should give our enemies agape. Do you need to give someone agape although they don't deserve it? What will you do to give this person *agape*?

BREAKING THE HUDDLE

The Importance of Relationships
Ephesians 5:8-33; Proverbs 3:5-6

> IN SPIRITUAL GROWTH,
> BE IT INDIVIDUAL
> OR CHURCH-WIDE,
> THE WORD
> "RELATIONSHIP"
> IS SECOND ONLY TO
> THE WORD "GOSPEL."

"COMMUNITY TIME"
IN MINISTRY

The most important thing we do in life is centered on building relationships. The first chapter of *Faithful Over A Few Things* is entitled "Nurturing and Cherishing Relationships." It is not by accident that chapter came first! In spiritual growth, be it individual or church-wide, the word "relationship" is second only to the word "gospel." You may disagree, but cherishing and nurturing a relationship is a lot easier to say than to do.

One thing you can do to build relationships in the church is to include "community time" in all ministries, auxiliaries, committees, leadership groups and staff meetings. After prayer and Scripture reading, but before the business agenda, spend thirty minutes or more gathered into small groups, discussing anything except church business. Focus on strengthening and building inter-

> WE NEED COMMUNITY TIME IN THE CHURCH BECAUSE WE GET SO BUSY DOING CHURCH BUSINESS THAT OUR RELATIONSHIPS BREAK DOWN FROM THE WEAR AND TEAR OF MINISTRY.

personal relationships. Share your joys and concerns with each other. Get to know each other better.

Allow at least the first thirty minutes or so to "community time" but don't be surprised if it lasts longer! In one deacons' meeting at our church, what was planned as thirty minutes of community time actually lasted for ninety minutes! It was not on our agenda, but we needed that much time to build and strengthen relationships.

We need community time in the church because we get so busy doing church business that our relationships break down from the wear and tear of ministry. I often say that I really don't consider myself to have any enemies, but I am fully aware that I have some confused friends in the church. Community time is a good time to clear up misunderstandings between brothers and sisters working together in ministry.

People often may be hurt or offended by things you didn't even know anything about! We need to know if we have inadvertently hurt or offended someone. I know I do! If I have offended someone, I want to restore that relationship. I *want* to beg their pardon! Community time gives me the opportunity to do that. It gives us the opportunity to know each other outside of church work. Community time helps us rejoice with each other over the victories and comfort each other in sorrow. It really takes time to build, cherish and nurture relationships between the members and the pastor and among the members themselves so we can have healthy interaction between the church and society at-large.

BEING CHILDREN OF LIGHT

Our Scripture in Ephesians 5:8 says that we Christians ought to walk in the light. "We were once in darkness, but now we are in the light of the Lord. Walk as children of light." We are to build our Christian relationships with a spirit of illumination, with a spirit of light. That simply means that we cannot lean on our own understanding. Too many of us are leaning on our own understanding, and when we do that, we are walking in darkness.

> THE MOST CRITICAL RELATIONSHIPS WE HAVE INCLUDE OUR RELATIONSHIP WITH GOD, WITH OTHER CHURCH MEMBERS, WITH OUR SPOUSES, WITH OUR CHILDREN, AND OUR RELATIONSHIPS WITH OUR CO-WORKERS ...

Proverbs 3:5-6 says, "Trust in the Lord with all thine heart and lean not to your own understanding. In all your ways acknowledge Him, and He shall direct your path."

What does that mean? That means that we don't walk with each other according to reason or logic. If you have a B.A., M.A. or Ph.D., you may be tempted to walk according to your own understanding, but you need to walk according to the light. Wherever the light shines is where you should walk. Using reason or logic to build, cherish and nurture relationships isn't effective. We ought to be children of the light. The most critical relationships we have include our relationship with God, with other church members, with our spouses, with

> A CHRISTIAN'S DUTY
> IS TO BE FILLED WITH
> THE SPIRIT BECAUSE
> IT IS THE SPIRIT THAT
> HELPS US BUILD,
> CHERISH AND
> NURTURE
> RELATIONSHIPS.

our children, and with our co-workers – whether they be above, beside or below us in authority. Many of us live crisis-ridden, broken lives because we are dealing with other people in our own understanding. Let's walk in the light instead of darkness.

BE FILLED WITH THE SPIRIT

What does God say that will help us walk in the light? In Ephesians 5:17, the Bible says, "Wherefore be ye not unwise..." In other words, "Don't be foolish!" That's my translation. "...but understanding what the will of the Lord is. And be not drunk with wine, wherein is excess; but be filled with the Spirit; Speaking to yourselves in psalms and hymns and spiritual songs, singing and making melody in your heart to the Lord; giving thanks for all things unto God and the Father in the name of our Lord Jesus Christ; submitting yourselves one to another in the fear of God."

A Christian's duty is to be filled with the Spirit because it is the Spirit that helps us to build, cherish and nurture relationships. The tense of this verse is present plural, indicating a continual process – it is not a one time filling. You received the Spirit at salvation, but the call on your life is to be *continuously filled* as you are going. Be filled with the Spirit and don't be foolish about it as you go!

This same passage says that it is just as bad to be intoxicated as to be unfilled. Church members wouldn't tolerate a preacher who came in the pulpit drunk on Sunday morning. They would run him out! Yet, if he came unfulfilled in relationships, they likely wouldn't say a word. Church members won't tolerate a drunk deacon or trustee – not for one minute! They would demand their removal! Yet, deacons and trustees walk unfulfilled in relationships all the time and no one cares. This passage applies to every Christian. "Don't be drunk in excess with wine, but be filled with the Spirit!" We put too much emphasis on avoiding the drunkenness and not enough on the filling of the Spirit.

> WE PUT TOO MUCH EMPHASIS ON AVOIDING DRUNKENNESS AND NOT ENOUGH ON THE FILLING OF THE SPIRIT.

EVIDENCE OF BEING FILLED

What is the evidence of a Spirit-filled life? One who is filled with the Spirit has a spirit of singing. "Speak to one another with songs, hymns and spiritual songs. Sing and make music in your heart to the Lord …" (Ephesians 5:19, NIV). A Spirit-filled person has a spirit of thankfulness. A Spirit-filled person is just thankful to be alive! Complaining, criticizing and worrying are not evidence of being Spirit-filled. You have joy when your cup runneth over with the Holy Spirit! It doesn't matter what your situation is, if you are filled with the Spirit, you will have a thankful spirit.

Another indication of a Spirit-filled life is submissiveness one to another. Some of us don't want to be submissive to anything or anyone because it is contrary to the way the world walks! Submissiveness is contrary to darkness. If we are going to be children of light, we must be submissive to each other. A spirit of singing, thankfulness and submissiveness is like fertil-

> SUBMISSIVENESS BETWEEN EQUALS CREATES HARMONY IN THE FAMILY AS IT DOES WITH CHRIST AND THE CHURCH.

izer for growing Christ-like relationships.

God says, "wives, be submissive to your husband," and many people want to stop reading right there because we don't understand what it really means. We want to walk according to our opinions on how marriage should work. God didn't ask for our opinion! His Word says, "wives, be submissive to your husbands!" Understand that this is willing submissiveness. It cannot be forced by the husband or anyone else. This is submissiveness between equals. It has nothing to do with superiority or inferiority. Submissiveness between equals creates harmony in the family as it does with Christ and the Church.

Spirit-filled husbands are supposed to love their wives just as Christ loved the Church. How much did Christ love the Church? He gave His life for her to clean her up and make her spotless, without a wrinkle! He loved the Church even more than He loved His own body. Spirit-filled men should love their wives as much as Christ loved the Church and as much as they love their own bodies.

We men love our bodies and we love ourselves! Men, if you don't believe we males love ourselves, let me put you to the test. Suppose I show you a photo of twenty people. If you are in that picture, who will you look for first? You look for yourself! You keep your eyes on yourself! Why would you do that? Because you love yourself! You need to love your wife as much as you love yourself! That's evidence of a Spirit-filled man.

That's a man who will cherish and nurture his marriage. This is a real mystery that cannot be understood with logic and reason. When a husband and wife are willing to be Spirit-controlled and walk in the light, they will find fulfillment they never knew before.

A man and a woman should leave their parents and cleave one to the other. Cleave means "to be stuck like glue." When you marry, you are to leave your parents and cleave to each other. The reason so many marriages fail is that we have too many men who are "momma's boys" and too many women who are "daddy's little girls." Every time something happens, daughters want to run back and be daddy's little girl and sons want to run to momma because they are still momma's boys. Men, when you get married, you aren't "momma's little boy" anymore, and that makes a lot of mothers sad. Leave them alone, momma, because they are married and have a wife! Leave them alone daddy, because they have a husband now. They are to cleave to each other, to be glued one to the other.

> ... IN BUILDING RELATIONSHIPS, THE GREATER BURDEN IS ALWAYS ON THE ONE WHO IS THE HEAD.

WALK IN THE LIGHT AS PARENTS

We must walk in the light in our relationships with our children as well as with our spouse. Children are to obey their parents, but the burden of responsibility for successful relationships between parents and children always lies with the head.

Parents, do not provoke your children! Just because your momma and daddy provoked you doesn't mean you should provoke your own children now! How many of you have asked your

GOD GIVES US
A WORD FOR
BUILDING,
CHERISHING, AND
NURTURING
RELATIONSHIPS
AT WORK.

child, "I guess I'm a liar, huh?" I don't care if your momma said that to you! That was then, and this is now. We can break the cycle of parenting like we were raised if it was unhealthy and provoking. We can be different than our parents. If you catch your children lying, getting in their face and saying, "I guess I'm a liar, huh?" doesn't teach them anything, and it damages your relationship. That's provoking. It's negative, and that's not what God would have us to do with our children. We must walk in the light with them by being loving teachers. By doing so, we can shape our children's behavior and build a healthy relationship at the same time.

WALK IN THE LIGHT AT WORK

God gives us a word for building, cherishing, and nurturing relationships at work. It doesn't matter if you are the supervisor or the subordinate, whether you're in charge or under authority – it's still pretty simple. If you are the employee, you are to respect your supervisor with fear and trembling. That doesn't mean that you shake and scratch your head. It means that you have respect for those in authority over you. One of the reasons many of us have so much anxiety on the job is that we like to think we can do the job better than our supervisor. It is hard to respect our supervisors because the natural man in us resists being under the authority of anyone. We think to ourselves, "Who does he think he is? I can do this job better than he can anyway!"

Be filled with the Spirit and walk in the light toward those over you at work. You could be a powerful witness leading an unsaved supervisor to a relationship with Jesus. Children, walk in the light and lean not on your own understanding!

If you are in authority over others at work, remember that in relationship-building, the greater burden is always on the one who is the head. Don't threaten or provoke your employees! Some of us get drunk with power when we get into a supervisory position. We call a meeting every morning with the attitude, "Some heads are going to roll around here!" We try to make people straighten up by threatening them or having staff meetings at the worst time of day, just to assert our authority over our employees. Employers and managers, you have a responsibility. If you are a supervisor or a business owner, you need to understand one thing – everybody ultimately has the same Master, God Himself!

> WE SHOULD ALL BE SUBMISSIVE ONE TO EACH OTHER BECAUSE WE ARE ALL UNDER THE AUTHORITY OF THE ONE TRUE LIVING GOD.

RELATIONSHIPS ARE OUR PRIORITY

We should all be submissive one to each other because we are all under the authority of the one true living God. External factors like educational level or salary or job title don't matter; we all must be submissive to each other if we want to walk in the light as children of God who serve the same master. Walk not according to your own understanding, but walk according to the Word of God with the Spirit of illumination, with a heart that

> LOVE AND
> RELATIONSHIPS
> ARE THE MOST
> ESSENTIAL THINGS
> IN LIFE SO GIVE
> THEM PRIME TIME.

truly wants to build cherishing and nurturing relationships with the people in your life.

Relationships should be given prime time. These are some evil times in which we live, so redeem it as best you can. Redeeming the time doesn't mean you can buy it back. It means you better capture the time you do have and not waste it on worthless activity. Love and relationships are the most essential things in life so give them prime time. Institute community time in your church. Community time must be practiced as much as choir practice, communion rehearsal, Sunday School instruction, and other kinds of church activities. Relationships have got to be given prime time because they make church work rewarding, and help members prevent burn out.

Don't just be a Christian, be a Spirit-filled Christian who walks in the light. Finally, the point isn't simply whether or not we have the Holy Spirit. The real question is, how much does the Holy Spirit have us? Are you submissive to the Holy Spirit? What percentage of you does the Holy Spirit own? If it isn't 100 percent, you need to increase your submissiveness to Him. Can you really say you have surrendered all to Him freely?

> ULTIMATELY,
> LOVING
> RELATIONSHIPS ARE
> THE ONLY THINGS
> THAT MAKE LIFE
> WORTH LIVING.

Loving relationships are more important than anything else. Ultimately, loving relationships are the only things that make life worth living. If you want Christ-like relationships in your life, I encourage you to live according to the Word and walk in the light. It all starts with a continual filling of the Holy Spirit that comes when you totally and completely submit yourself to Him, admitting that you are powerless to walk in the light according to your own understanding.

Give yourself over to the Holy Spirit right now. Pray, "Lord, help me now to give myself to you. Holy Spirit pray for me that I will surrender all; that I will be submissive and obedient as a child of God. Whatever You need to do in my life ... do it! If it means making me all over, make me all over. If it means breaking me, I thank You for the brokenness and the restoration that will follow. I thank you for being Father; now help me to be Your child. Help me to know and apply the most essential principle of growing the Church – building, cherishing and nurturing relationships in my life. Help me to be a doer of the Word, and not a hearer only."

CHAPTER FOUR
STUDY GUIDE

1. Define "community time" :

2. Fill in the blanks:

    _____ is second only

    to _____.

    People often may be _____ or

    _____ by things

    _____!

3. How can community time help your church cherish and nurture relationships?

4. Read Ephesians 5:8. Compare and contrast walking in darkness with walking in the light.

5. Read Proverbs 3:5-6. Why is it so hard for us to trust the Lord and not our own understanding in our relationship with other people?

6. Describe two ways evidence of a spirit filled life is demonstrated.

7. Ephesians 5:21-33 tells us that godly marriage is submissiveness between equals. Define equal submissiveness in your own words.

8. Fill in the blanks:

   Parents don't _____ your children!

   We can break _____ like we were raised if it _____.

   We can be _____ than our parents.

9. Who has the strongest burden in building a relationship?

10. What does it mean to walk in the light as a supervisor at work?

11. How can you walk in the light as an employee under authority on your job?

For Deeper Study

1. Read James 3:1-18. What behavior is the subject of this passage? How can this behavior help or hinder walking in the light in your relationships?

2. Read Psalm 37:3-5. What are the desires of your heart? Name three things you need to commit to the Lord in relationships.

Huddle Group Discussion

1. Discuss why in relationships it is difficult for you to walk in the light. Be honest!

2. What do you think about adding community time to the busy ministry schedule? Would you be willing to try it? Explain.

3. On a 1-10 scale, to what degree is cherishing and nurturing relationships a priority in your church?

Break the Huddle!

Think about the key points of this message and how they apply to the most difficult relationship in your life. What will you do differently to walk in the light in this relationship?

BREAKING THE HUDDLE

Evangelize in Deep Water
Luke 5:1-11

THE MAJORITY
OF UNCONFESSED
SINNERS ... ARE
OUT WHERE THE
WATER IS DEEP...

WE OUGHT TO PUSH OUT

One of the problems with the church today is that we want to stay in shallow water. The Bible, without question, tells us that we ought to push out into deep waters. When you break the huddle, you have to go out farther. Why? The majority of unconfessed sinners are not in church. Where are they? They are somewhere out where the water is deep, so we ought to push out into deeper water. Jesus has commanded us through His Great Commission: "Go ye therefore, and teach all nations, baptizing them in the name of the Father, and of the Son and of the Holy Ghost," (Matthew 28:19). God told us to go, and we can depend on His promise that He will be with us – even in deep water.

In Luke 5:1-11, Jesus confronted some fishermen washing their nets. Jesus got in their boat and invited the fishermen to

> ALTHOUGH WE KNOW THE MAGNIFICENCE OF GOD, SOMETIMES GOD DOES SOMETHING SO POWERFUL, SO MIRACULOUS, THAT WE ARE IN AWE OF HIM.

get in with Him. Jesus then sat down and taught them. The Bible says that after He had finished teaching them, He told them to push out a little bit farther and let down their nets. One of the fishermen, Simon, gave this kind of answer, "Lord, we're tired. We have been toiling all night and haven't caught anything." As I imagine the situation, I think he probably also said, "It is the heat of the day, and fish don't bite when it is hot. It's off-season. We're not going to catch any fish now." But Simon also said, "By thy Word, I will go out a little deeper."

Then Jesus said, "Now let down your net." After they lowered their net and pulled it in, the Bible says that they caught so many fish that they had to call in other boats to help. The fishermen were awestruck at their enormous catch.

IN AWE OF HIM

When God does something wonderful, it makes us feel so unworthy – which we are. Although we know the magnificence of God, sometimes God does something so powerful, so miraculous, that we are in awe of Him. Peter was a professional fisherman. He knew that fish are generally not caught in the middle of the day. It was also hot and it was the off season. Yet they had so many fish! The power of Christ often defies what our eyes can see and what our minds can understand. Peter had been fishing all night and hadn't caught a thing. After following the Master's instructions, he caught so many fish that his net was breaking. He was so awestruck that he fell down worshiping Jesus, saying, "Depart from me. I am not even worthy to be in your presence."

Jesus, knowing all of Peter's unworthiness, replied, "Fear not, for this is your last day fishing for fish. I am going to make you a fisher of men. From this day forth, you will catch men and women for me." Peter and his

> WE DON'T WANT
> TO FISH WAY
> OUT BECAUSE WE
> KNOW THERE IS
> TOO MUCH DANGER
> OUT THERE IN
> THE DEEP WATER!

fishing partners put down their fish and their fishing equipment, picked up the cross of Jesus, and followed him to become fishers of men and women.

THE CHURCH IS "BANK FISHING"

As fishers of men and women, the church has a problem. We do too much "bank fishing." We fish from the dock, and if the dock goes out into the water, we'll sit on the edge of the dock, but that's as far as we'll go. We don't want to fish way out because we know there is too much danger out there in the deep water! Sharks and all kinds of strange fish live way out in deep water.

I used to go deep-sea fishing in Florida. Every once in a while we would catch a stingray, which is poisonous. The captain would stop the ship and use some long shears to cut the stingray loose. Sometimes it doesn't matter how much you want to reel the catch in, you have to give up your line, sink, hooks and all. You don't want to reel in a stingray! You find dangerous fish like that in deep water.

Some of us are afraid to go into deep water because of the sharks and stingrays. If you go out into deep water, somebody

> NOT ONLY
> IS THE CHURCH
> FISHING FROM
> THE BANK, BUT
> WE ARE ALSO
> DOING TOO MUCH
> "POLE FISHING."

might curse you out. If you go to the inner city, people might smell bad or look scary. If you take the gospel inside a gay bar, the folks might laugh at you or mistake you for being gay just because you're there. If you go fishing for Jesus in an AIDS hospice, you may be asked to hug someone who needs your touch before dying alone. If you go out fishing for Jesus on death row, you may find yourself reeling in a murderer or a serial killer. If you go out in deep water to tell someone about Jesus, you may not be able to repeat what they say to you. I propose there is no real danger in the deep water if you remain in Jesus' boat. There is a song entitled "The Old Ship of Zion" with lyrics that read, "Ain't no danger in the water … She has landed many a thousand …Get on board, get on board." If we're in the ship with Jesus, trusting Jesus, with our eyes on Jesus, He will help us catch the strange fish and bring them in. Break the huddle and go fishing with Jesus!

TOO MUCH "POLE FISHING"

It matters how you fish. Not only is the church fishing from the bank, but we are also doing too much "pole fishing." We are still using things like country cane poles or tree branches. When you're fishing with a pole, there is only one guarantee – you won't catch but one fish at a time! Pole fishing is a very, very slow process.

Some fishermen have graduated to fishing with a rod and reel, which are supposed to get your bait a little farther out in the water – but you still only catch one fish at a time.

Jesus said, "Cast your net." Jesus didn't believe in bank fishing, dock fishing, pole fishing, or rod-and-reel fishing. Jesus believed in fishing with a net in a boat that was going somewhere. Most of us, however, like our comfort zones! We prefer to fish discriminately with a pole so we can catch just the kind of fish we want to catch in comfort. We want to catch a fish that looks like us … that smells like us … that dresses like us … fish with similar education and financial resources. That is what's wrong with the church today – too much pole fishing from comfort zones.

> GOD WILL TAKE CARE OF US WHILE WE ARE OUT IN DEEP WATER BECAUSE WE HAVE DONE WHAT HE HAS ORDERED US TO DO.

Once I attended an evangelism workshop, and the teacher taught us that the best way to target our primary audience in ministry is homogeneously. Find out what you are like, then go out and find those who are just like you. He said that is called "effective target evangelism." Although I realize that target evangelism does have its value and place, I had to raise my hand and respond by saying that might be true, but it is not a truth. Some things may be true, but they are not truths. It is true that people like to go to church with people who are like them, but that doesn't make it a biblical truth.

God wants us to fish in deep water with a big net. God will take care of us while we are out in deep water because we have done what He has ordered us to do. Trials and frustrations may occur when we try to tame a shark or pull in a big scavenger fish, but God wants us out there pulling in everybody. Break the huddle because He wants us net fishing in deep water!

A Certain Kind of Bait

It matters what kind of bait, depending on the type of fish you want to catch. You can use worms, crickets, minnows, or dough bread, like my daddy used to use. What do you fish with? If you fish with a worm, you'll catch a certain kind of fish. If you fish with crickets, you'll catch a different kind of fish. If you fish with minnows, you'll catch fish that like minnows. If you fish with artificial bait, you'll catch other kinds of fish.

> The only real bait ... is the saving knowledge of Jesus, which is in the Word of God.

I suspect that many of us are not only pole fishing, but we are fishing with a certain kind of bait. Some of us are fishing with, "We-get-out-in-one-hour" bait; we lure people in by telling them how short the worship service is. Some of us are fishing with "choir" bait; we tell our friends, "You ought to hear our choir." Some of us are fishing with society bait; we attract people because the members of our church are in high society. The only real bait, however, is the saving knowledge of Jesus, which is in the Word of God.

Break the huddle and push out! Push out into deep waters. Push out in the Old Ship of Zion, which is a ship representing a type of Christ. Noah's ark was a type of Christ because it had saving power. And this ship, the Old Ship of Zion, is a type of Christ. Troubles don't exist in the water, because she has landed many a thousand. Break the huddle and get on board!

The Church Has to Break the Huddle

Let's look at some spiritual truths related to fishing. The first truth is that the boat must get off the dock. The church as a whole has to break the huddle, not just a few members of the church. In Luke 5:1-11, we read that Jesus walked up to the boat and found it anchored to the dock. You can't catch anything if you are anchored to the dock! We need to be out fishing for homeless people living under the bridge. The Church needs to sail into uncharted territory like Alcoholics Anonymous meetings, crack houses and red light districts.

SOME OF US ARE NET-WASHERS ... WE PREPARE TO FISH BUT WE NEVER ACTUALLY DO ANY FISHING.

A second truth is that we have to follow God's time line, not our own! When I was preparing to go salmon fishing in San Francisco, I didn't have the right time frame of mind. I thought we were just going out to fish for a short while. When I told the captain what time I had to get back, he told me that we'd never make it in time because it took an hour to get out where we are going to fish, and an hour to get back. I thought we were going out for about thirty minutes and catch some fish but it took an hour just to get started! That's deep water. If we are to be effective witnesses, we must break the huddle, evangelize in deep water, and be willing to let God move in His time.

Third, fishing nets are not meant to be washed. They are meant for fishing! The fishermen in our text were washing their nets. Some of us are net-washers. In other words, we prepare to fish, but we never actually do any fishing. We are polishing our cane poles, oiling our rods and reels, going to workshops, and studying. We are preparing, trying to memorize Scriptures, and going to soul-winning workshops. There is nothing wrong with preparing; however, the Bible didn't say to go to ten workshops in a year. The Word of God instructs us

> THE HOLY SPIRIT HAS EVERYTHING READY NOW! IT'S TIME FOR DEEP WATER. GO! BREAK THE HUDDLE!

to, "Break the huddle and go!" We don't need to sit around for a year polishing up our rods and reels, washing our nets, dealing with our cane poles, or checking our bait.

The Holy Spirit has everything ready now! It's time for deep water. Go! Break the huddle! Push out! Evangelize in deep water, and go a little farther!

GET IN THE SHIP AND STAY WITH JESUS

Not only must the ship push out from the dock, but you must get in the ship. Jesus invited them to *get in* the ship *with* Him. You go to church every Sunday, but are you really in the ship! Some are not! You may be a member of the church, but you aren't really in the ship. The ship has to do the work of evangelism. You're singing in the choir, and that's good ... but are you in the ship? Every choir member, every usher, every deacon, every trustee, every member of the church ought to be doing what Jesus said to do in His very last commandment, "Go ye therefore, and teach all nations, ..." Get in the ship and go somewhere with Jesus!

When you get in the ship, stay in the ship. Don't abandon it. The captain is supposed to be the last one to abandon the ship. All of us are captains because we belong to the priesthood of believers. In the book of Acts (27:31), when Paul was shipwrecked, the main thing the sailors were told was to stay with the ship. Even after the ship was broken into pieces, they were told to hold on to a broken piece of the ship. God can take our broken pieces, and with the brokenness of Calvary, He can still get us to dry land if we hold on. Don't jump out of the ship! Don't leave the church in adverse circumstances!

While you're sailing on the ship, always keep Jesus in the ship with you. I have concerns about events like the Million Man March because it caused some to jump ship and leave Jesus behind.

> DON'T JUMP SHIP!
> STAY ON BOARD
> AND KEEP JESUS
> IN THE SHIP
> WITH YOU.

As noble as any cause may be, believers must make sure Jesus is on that ship. It may be tempting to align ourselves with "good" causes, but we cannot put a bandage on the sins of our nation in an effort of heal or correct them.

Don't jump ship! Stay on board and keep Jesus in the ship with you.

BE OBEDIENT

How many times does God need to tell you to be a witness? How often have you been obedient to His call to witness? Opportunities to witness are everywhere! You can be a witness on your job, at home, at the store, and in the community.

How many times does God have to ask you before you obey His will? Break the huddle! Cast out. Push out a little bit farther. How many times does God have to say that? When He said it to Simon, he made excuses to Jesus. Many of us can be quite creative in coming up with excuses to disobey Him. "I'm too busy," or "I don't have enough scriptural knowledge." Other excuses might be, "I've never been in a prison," or "I don't know what to say to a drug addict."

Simon probably said something akin to, "I'm tired. I've been fishing all night. I worked a double shift. I worked all night and still I don't have anything." God wants obedience and we give Him excuses. Be obedient! Try Him and see if He will not open up the windows of heaven and pour you out a blessing. How many times does Jesus have to say whatever He is saying to us before we become willing to do it?

No excuses are acceptable, not even "I'm still behind on my bills" … "My marriage is on the rocks" … "Homosexuality makes me sick on my stomach" … "I'm afraid to go in those housing projects" … "My boss is making my life miserable!" Simon changed his course and decided to break the huddle in obedience. Why? "Because of thy Word I will do it."

The only reason Simon was obedient and pushed out was because the Word of God said to do so. He broke the huddle, cast out in deep water, and let the nets down.

GET ON THE RIGHT SIDE

I believe that Simon and the other fishermen let the net down on the "right side." There is something powerful about being on the "right side." Jesus is sitting on the right hand of God the Father Almighty. The Psalmist says, "Thy right hand holds me." Remember the parable of the goats and the sheep? (Matthew 25:32-46) Jesus said at the end of time there will be a division of nations, with the goats on the left and the sheep on the right.

Those on the left are those who were not obedient to the Word. They didn't feed the hungry, evangelize, clothe the naked, or visit the sick. Jesus will say to the goats on the left, "Depart from me." But to those on the right He will say, "Enter now into the joy of your reward. You have been faithful over a few things, now I will make you ruler and master over many." Cast your net on the right, and get right! When the disciples got right, the net was full of salvation and blessings.

Many of us today are like Simon. We are astounded that God could save a someone like us and work a miracle through our life – but He can! I don't care what you've done, or where your hands have been –by the righteousness of God living in you, you can lift up clean, holy hands before Him. Simon said, "Depart from me," and Jesus said, "Fear not, because I can make you holy. I'm going to make you a fisher of men." The Bible says that they broke the huddle and cast their nets in deep water.

WILL YOU BE A DEEP SEA FISHERMAN?

Have you been fishing all night without catching a thing? Are you sure you are fishing like Jesus would? Are you pole fishing on the bank in comfort with a certain kind of bait? Have you caught anything lately for God? Would you like to be more successful at fishing? Be encouraged!

You can make a decision right now to be obedient and evangelize in deep water with a net. You will probably find a few sting rays or sharks in the net, but you won't have to cut them loose if you have Jesus in the boat with you. He's an expert at catching stingrays and sharks. He will guide your way and show you just what to do!

CHAPTER FIVE
STUDY GUIDE

1. Why do we need to be fishing for men outside the church?

2. Why does the water get deeper the further away from the church you go?

3. How is the church "bank fishing?" Is it possible to fish in the deepest water from the bank?

4. If you really evangelize in deep water, you might catch a stingray or a shark. What is one kind of person you avoid fishing for? Why would you hesitate to pull that fish in your boat?

5. Define how the church goes "pole fishing."

6. What kind of "bait" attracted you to your church?

7. Identify the kinds of "bait" you use when you invite people to come to church?

8. Name the only bait that can be used effectively to fish in every church.

9. What does being a net-washer mean? Are you a net washer or a net user?

10. Why is it important to keep Jesus in the ship with you? What happens when people go fishing without Him?

FOR DEEPER STUDY

1. Read Matthew 9:10-13. How was Jesus evangelizing in deep water?

2. Read Matthew 18:10-13. How is the one lost sheep that was found like a shark or stingray out in the deep water?

HUDDLE GROUP DISCUSSION

1. Can you think of some fish that your church is not trying to catch? Be honest! Who is out too deep for your congregation?

2. What "bait" is your church known for? Should you add more variety on your hook?

3. Would you say your church is fishing with a pole or a net?

BREAK THE HUDDLE!

In review question four, you identified a kind of person you avoid fishing for. What fear or repulsion will you work to overcome so you might be able to catch a fish like that someday?

BREAKING THE HUDDLE

6

Just Can't Keep It to Myself
Acts 4:7-20; Jeremiah 20:9

JUST CAN'T SHUT UP

I don't know about you, but God has been good to me, and I just can't keep it to myself. When you can't keep it to yourself, you are compelled to break the huddle and tell someone about Jesus and what He did for you on the cross. Two scriptures – one from the Old Testament and one from the New – give examples of those who came before us who just couldn't keep it to themselves.

From the book of Jeremiah we know that Jeremiah was the prophet who was called from his mother's womb to tell what thus saith the Lord. He was very young when God called him to begin prophesying and preaching. During his lifetime, he prophesied to five different kings of Judah. Jeremiah was preaching God's Word with such power that the chief of the Temple began ridiculing him then had him whipped. Isn't it

GOD WANTS A
CHRISTIAN ON
FIRE, BECAUSE HE
USES HOT STUFF TO
DISPLAY POWER.

interesting? God always has a problem with religious people. The only people Jesus really had a problem with were the religious people of His day. How frustrating it must have been to be a prophet in those days! Jeremiah took the whipping but afterwards complained to God for even being born. In Jeremiah 20:9, he said, "I will not make mention of him, nor speak anymore in his name. But his word was in mine heart as a burning fire shut up in my bones, and I was weary with, and I could not stay." He wanted to stop talking about God, but he just couldn't do it.

CATCH ON FIRE

Think about what it means to feel like fire is shut up in your bones. Some time ago, the dairy across the street from our church caught on fire, and we couldn't get out of our driveway. The fire was so intense that we could hear it flaming and burning. Think about that kind of flame shut up in your bones! Jeremiah just couldn't keep it to himself!

Isn't it is interesting how God uses hot stuff all through the Bible? God wants a Christian on fire, because He uses hot stuff to display power. He used fire on the Day of Pentecost to usher in His church when the Holy Spirit descended on the believers. He used hot stuff when He called Isaiah to be His servant.

In Isaiah 6:5, Isaiah said, "Woe unto me! I am a man of unclean lips and I am among a people who are unclean." Then one of the seraphim flew down to the altar, picked up a hot coal and purged him of his iniquity by placing it on his tongue. Then in verse eight, Isaiah was ready to answer God's call, "Here I am, send me."

The Lord uses fire and hot stuff. He's got some hot stuff that He's prepared for the devil, called the lake of fire. The Bible says it wasn't prepared for you, but it was prepared for the devil and his angels. Those who choose

THE CHURCH NEEDS TO CATCH ON FIRE FOR SHARING JESUS.

not to accept the Lord will be going where there is plenty of fire and hot stuff. God doesn't want you to suffer – He wants you to be blessed by His good hot stuff. He wants you to catch on fire and glorify Him.

The Church needs to catch on fire for sharing Jesus. If He's been good to you, you ought to share Him with others. Everywhere you go, you ought to talk about Him. In the grocery store, on your job or in a restaurant, you need to tell someone about the gospel. You need to break the huddle by catching on fire and running through the streets for Jesus.

One of the nicest compliments that I have ever been given as a preacher came early in my pastorate. We were a small church at that time, and a brother who had been coming to church regularly met me after service at the door. I remember shaking his hand and asking him how he was doing. Most people respond, "fine," just making small talk. This man was honest and admitted he wasn't doing very well, despite the fact that he had all the trappings of material, worldly success. So I asked him, "Well, have you been enjoying the sermons? (What a bold question for a preacher to ask!) He said, "I haven't heard a word you said." I became curiously concerned and asked, "Well, brother, why do you keep coming every Sunday?" He replied, "I just come to see you catch on fire. I just don't believe anybody can feel as good as you do. I cer-

> I DON'T CARE HOW MANY OR WHAT KINDS OF SIN YOU'VE COMMITTED – GOD IS ABLE!

tainly don't feel that good myself. I need to see somebody who feels as good as you say you feel. I just come here to watch you burn up every Sunday." What a compliment! I've been asking the Lord to let me burn up ever since!

ANOTHER BIBLICAL EXAMPLE

In the New Testament, we find a similar scenario involving Peter and John, after the Day of Pentecost. Peter was on fire even though he had denied Jesus in the Garden. Sometimes when you fall out of fellowship with God, you think you are locked out forever. But once reconciled with God through Jesus, God is always there waiting to forgive you because He is your Father.

I have three sons, and regardless of what they do, I am still their father. I can't change it and they can't change it either because we are bound together in a father/son relationship.

Peter was out of the fellowship for a while after he had denied Jesus in the Garden, but the Lord restored him by the Sea of Galilee. Peter, once backslidden and out of the fellowship, was now back in and full of the Holy Spirit. God can do it every time! Perhaps you have a relationship with God, but you've been out of the fellowship. I don't care how far you sink out of the fellowship; I don't care how many or what kinds of sin you've committed – God is able! Peter preached at Pentecost, full of the Holy Ghost, and 3,000 people were saved, and the Lord added to the church daily. Peter was preaching his heart out!

In Acts 4:7-20, the religious folks were concerned because it was late in the evening and so many people were coming to the Lord; so they arrested Peter and John and put them in jail. The two were brought before the Sanhedrin, the religious order of the church, because a man had been saved and he had been running through God's house, leaping and jumping, praising God. The man had been running through the church like a fool. Have you ever seen anyone like that? A person can get so happy in Jesus that he will be running and praising God like a complete fool because he just can't keep it to himself.

> IF GOD HAS BEEN GOOD TO YOU, YOU MUST TELL SOMEBODY ABOUT WHAT YOU HAVE SEEN, FELT, AND HEARD.

Those religious folks, the Sanhedrin, asked, "By what name did this man get healed?" Peter told them that it was Jesus, saying, "There is no other name under heaven given among men whereby we must be saved." Peter was preaching Jesus crucified and resurrected! The religious folks looked at the disciples and then considered the man who had once been lame and now was healed. His healing could not be debated. They didn't have the power to put Peter and John to death so they called them outside and asked them to stop talking about Jesus. They just wanted them to be quiet. Peter and John said, "Judge for yourself whether it is right in God's sight to obey you or to obey Him; for we cannot help speaking about what we have seen and heard." They just couldn't keep it to themselves. They had to break the huddle with the religious folks! If God has been good to you, you must tell somebody about what you have seen, felt, and heard.

MAKE IT PUBLIC

Each of us should be able to identify with Peter and John because surely God has been good to us. We should be on fire for the Lord! We should burst out of the huddle, telling people about our salvation experience. God asks that we make *public* what He has done for us in *private*. We cannot hide behind the idea that we have a "personal relationship" with Him. That is good, but that's not all! Our relationship is personal, but what He can do and what He has done for us must be made public.

> OUR RELATIONSHIP IS PERSONAL, BUT WHAT HE CAN DO AND WHAT HE HAS DONE FOR US MUST BE MADE PUBLIC.

Why do we have a problem with this? It's certainly not because we lack communication skills. We get into huddles with other people and talk about everything but the right thing. We can talk about sports. We can talk about politics. We can talk about the soap operas on TV. We can even talk about the personalities on the soap operas as if we know them personally! We now can communicate on the Internet from one side of the world to the other! Someone once said that the three fastest modes of communication are telephone, telegraph and tell-a-saint. Our church grapevine can compete with the Internet! So why can't we talk about Jesus?

DO YOU BELIEVE IN HELL?

I think one of the reasons we don't talk more about Jesus is because we have a 20th Century mindset, and we don't believe in the reality of hell. I think our modern-day thinking prohibits people from believing that hell exists. You remember the parable of the rich man and poor Lazarus? They both died and the rich man went to hell while poor Lazarus went to heaven. The rich man in hell called out because of the torture. Be aware that those who go to hell will have feelings! The Bible says he was hot. God was using hot stuff on him, not good hot stuff, but bad hot stuff. It was worse than having somebody pour hot grits on you because hell is hotter than the hottest grits. Now that's hot!

ONCE YOU'RE IN HELL, YOU'LL NEVER HAVE ANOTHER OPPORTUNITY TO BREAK THE HUDDLE AGAIN.

The rich man called out for the poor beggar to come out of heaven to drop some water on his tongue to cool him off. The man was in hell, but still arrogant. Then he said, "If you won't do that, Lord, just let me out of here because I have some brothers back home. If you let someone in hell go back to earth and witness, they won't want to come here." In return, God said, "No, you had Moses and you had the prophets. If your brothers won't listen to them, it won't help them for you to return." Hell is a place of no return. Once you're in hell, you'll never have another opportunity to break the huddle again. The game is over.

FILLING THE GOD HOLE

We need the Lord. We all have a God hole in us and, until it's filled, we won't be satisfied. We try to fill it with different things. We try to fill it with work, so we become workaholics. We try to fill it with education or our careers and achievements. Some try to fill that empty hole with sex, alcohol, or drugs, but they will never be satisfied because there is only one thing that will fit in the God-made hole – Jesus Christ, the risen Savior.

Fill the God hole up with God Almighty. He is the only one who can fill it up! Break the huddle of routine conversation and

> WHAT WE HAVE
> IS A LOVE PROBLEM.
> WE DON'T
> LOVE PERFECTLY.

share the gospel. I don't know about you, but I just can't keep it to myself!

Fear is the believer's Public Enemy Number One. Many of us don't share Jesus because we are scared of failure, ridicule, or rejection. However, the Bible says that perfect love casts out fear (I John 4:18). What we have is a love problem. We don't love perfectly. We don't love God perfectly so we don't love ourselves perfectly and we don't love others perfectly. If we had perfect love, we would have compassion and passion for the salvation of others.

LOVE PERFECTLY AND BE ON THE DREAM TEAM

Some of us need to break the huddle with our own peer group and develop perfect love for all of humanity while we still have time. Before we can love our fellow man, we must first love God. That's why God said in the First Commandment "First love *Me*. Love the Lord your God with all your heart, soul, and mind, then you can love your neighbor."

If you loved the world as God loved the world, you would overcome your fears and share Jesus because you just wouldn't be able to keep it to yourself.

We are responsible to love perfectly and catch on fire for Jesus, but He has not left us alone to burn up by ourselves. As a matter of fact, as players on "God's Dream Team," He has put us on the first string. He is the Master Coach! The Word is on the Dream Team; the Holy Spirit is on the Dream Team; and the empowered believer is on the Dream Team. The word compels, convicts, and draws people to Jesus. The Holy Spirit precedes the witness and empowers believers to go and make disciples. We should thank God for allowing us to be on the Dream Team. When we love perfectly and play our role on the Dream Team, the kingdom of God definitely wins every time!

> ... YOU MAY NOT BE ABLE TO REACH EVERYONE, BUT YOU CAN REACH SOMEONE.

THREE SPIRITUAL TRUTHS

There are three relevant spiritual truths that will help you catch on fire and break the huddle to make you the most effective witness you can be for the Lord. The first truth is that you may not be able to reach everyone, but you can reach someone. Share Jesus! Share the gospel in the marketplace. As you are going from place to place, tell people in your path about what you have seen, heard, and felt.

You have heard it said, "I'm just a nobody, trying to tell everybody, about Somebody who can save anybody." You might feel like that nobody is you. Everybody is the whole world; no one is left out. That Somebody is Jesus. At one time, that anybody was me. God is able to help you with His good hot stuff!

The second truth is that nobody can debate your testimony about Jesus. In Acts 4:14, the religious people saw that the man who had been crippled was now healed and they couldn't debate that. You don't have to memorize Scripture to share Jesus if you have a testimony. If you've been tested, you have a testimony. Just tell somebody what the Lord has done for you. No one can debate with me concerning what God has done for me. This is my story. This is my testimony.

The third truth is that if God has been good to you, you ought to say so. Christians need to break the huddle of silence. Peter and John said that they could not help speaking about what they had seen, heard, and felt. If God has saved your soul, you ought to want to tell someone. If God has healed your body like He healed mine, how can you keep it to yourself? If God has ever picked you up, turned you around and put your feet on solid ground, you ought to say so. In Psalm 30:11, David said, "Thou hath turned my mourning into dancing; thou hast put off my sackcloth and girded me with gladness to the end that my glory will sing his praise and not be silent." If God has ever done anything for you, your testimony should burn like fire shut up in your bones!

> IF GOD HAS EVER DONE ANYTHING FOR YOU, YOUR TESTIMONY SHOULD BURN LIKE FIRE SHUT UP IN YOUR BONES!

Does your testimony burn inside? Do you feel God's good hot stuff working on the inside of you, yearning to burst out like a fire blowing out of the walls of a building? Can you hear your testimony burning on the inside? Can you feel it? I can! I just can't keep it to myself! If your testimony has died down inside like an old fire, ask the Holy Spirit to fan the flames for you. As long as one tiny ember remains, God can fan it back to a roaring fire that cannot be held inside. You, too, will be saying, "I just can't keep it to myself!"

CHAPTER SIX
STUDY GUIDE

1. In Jeremiah 20:9, how did the prophet describe the urgency to prophesy?

2. Name three ways God uses "hot stuff" in the Bible to display power.

3. Describe how Peter and John just couldn't keep the gospel of Jesus Christ to themselves in Acts.

4. Fill in the blanks:

   (a) We should be _____ _____ for the Lord!

   (b) What He can do and what He has done for us must be _____ _____ .

5. Do you believe hell is real? Give reasons to support your answer.

6. Why do you think so many Twentieth Century people don't believe in the reality of hell?

7. List five things people use to fill their God-hole rather than Jesus.

8. Describe and give examples of three reasons many people don't share Jesus.

9. What is the first thing you must do to overcome your fears so you can share Jesus?

10. Identify and describe the three spiritual truths that will help you catch on fire and share Jesus.

FOR DEEPER STUDY

1. In Mark 1:40-45, Jesus healed the leper and told him to obey the law regarding his healing as outlined in Leviticus 14:1-20. But the man did not follow the law – he just couldn't keep it to himself! What is the significance of this man's disobedience, given that he was healed by Jesus?

2. Read Mark 16:1-20. Describe how the two women named Mary and the disciples worked through their hesitation to be able to "say so" about the Lord. What did it take for them? Compare that with what Jesus says in John 20:27-29, as it applies to us today.

HUDDLE GROUP DISCUSSION

1. Have you ever experienced a time when you just couldn't keep it to yourself? Share with the group how you just had to say so about the goodness of Jesus in your life.

2. How can you effectively present the reality of hell and its finality to unbelievers?

3. Describe someone you know who is on fire for the Lord. What affect does that person have on the people around him/her?

BREAK THE HUDDLE!

Someone you know needs to hear you "say so" about the Lord. Someone you know needs to see you catch on fire for God. Who is this person? When can you tell them what God has done for you?

Breaking the Huddle

Boldly Stepping Over the Line
Romans 1:16-17; Hebrews 4:16

I'd Rather Have Jesus

> I KNOW THAT
> I WOULD RATHER
> HAVE JESUS THAN
> SILVER OR GOLD.
> THINK ABOUT HOW
> MUCH BETTER THE
> WORLD WOULD
> BE IF EVERYBODY
> MEANT THAT...

I'm sure Paul would have said, "I'd rather have Jesus than silver or gold." I know that I would rather have Jesus than silver or gold. Think about how much better the world would be if everybody meant that, especially church members. Some of us do mean that when we say it. One of the things the church can do today is to encourage Christians to say what they mean and to mean what they say. This means stepping over the line of doubt, shame and timidity into the land of boldness and faith.

Paul was bold. Though he was beaten, persecuted, and kicked out of town, still he could say in Romans 1:16-17, "I am not ashamed of the gospel of Jesus Christ for it is the power of God unto salvation to every one that believeth, to the Jew first, and also to the Greeks. For therein is the righteousness of God revealed from faith to faith. As it is written, the just shall live by faith." Paul was a man of faith who was not ashamed to break from the Pharisaic huddle to declare that Jesus is Lord.

BIBLICAL BOLDNESS CAUSES US TO BREAK THE HUDDLE AND WIN VICTORIES FOR THE KINGDOM OF GOD.

BIBLICAL BOLDNESS

God speaks to us through Paul concerning boldness in Hebrews 4:16, "Therefore, let us come boldly unto the throne of grace that we might obtain mercy and find grace to find help in time of need." Have you ever thought much about biblical boldness? As Christians, we should have boldness in Jesus!

Biblical boldness causes us to break the huddle and win victories for the Kingdom of God. From Genesis to Revelation, the Bible admonishes us to be bold as children of God. Notice how God uses the theme of boldness throughout His Word:

- Proverb 28:1 "The wicked flee ... but the righteous are as *bold* as a lion."

- Mark 15:43 "Joseph of Arimathea ... went in *boldly* unto Pilate, and craved the body of Jesus."

- Acts 4:13 "Now when they saw the *boldness* of Peter and John, and perceived that they were unlearned and ignorant men, they marveled; and they took knowledge of them, that they had been with Jesus."

- 1 Timothy 3:13 "For they that have used the office of deacon well purchase to themselves … great *boldness* in the faith which is in Christ Jesus…"

- Hebrews 4:16 "Let us therefore come *boldly* unto the throne of grace, that we might obtain mercy, and find grace to help in time of need."

- Hebrews 13:6 "So that we may *boldly* say the Lord is my helper and I will not fear what man shall do unto me."

If we are to act boldly for God, why are we so timid and shy when it comes to talking about Jesus? We can talk boldly about everything but Jesus! When it comes to the entertainment world, we can talk boldly about movie stars and TV celebrities; but when it comes to talking about Jesus, we become inhibited. We brag on the accomplishments of professional sports teams like we had something to do with their success! Yet when it comes to Jesus, sometimes we don't seem to have much to say. I think the reason we are shy for Jesus is that many of us have not really stepped over the line. What do I mean by that?

HOW "BAD" ARE YOU?

I remember when I was a little boy we didn't want to be called "scared," or a "sissy," or a "mama's boy." As boys, we would do anything to prove that we weren't a sissy, a nerd, or a wimp. No one wanted to date or marry a nerd or a wimp, so we had to do things to make sure everybody understood that we were "bad." One of our most important displays of manhood was playing games to prove that we were tough.

One game we played was called "Cut the Grass." Groups of boys would play in the grass for hours (no equipment needed), attempting to throw each other down, the objective being to remain standing. If you were "bad," you could remain standing and demand others to "cut the grass" or be thrown down. We spent endless hours playing this game to determine who was the biggest and the "baddest" of all the boys.

The game I remember most, however, was called "Step Over the Line." Everybody played that. We would draw a line in the dirt with one foot and say, "If you think you're bad, step over the line!" It didn't matter if your nose was bleeding, if you were whipped up, crying, or scared, you would step over the line because you wanted to prove you were tough.

> GET BOLD FOR JESUS, STEP OVER THE LINE, AND BREAK THE HUDDLE WITH TIMID, SHY DISCIPLES.

STEP OVER THE LINE FOR JESUS

It is time for somebody to step over the line for Jesus. We need to step over the line of religion into the land of the anointed and be filled with the Holy Ghost. We need to step over the line of church membership into the land of baptized believers. Pew sitters need to step over the line into a land of commitment.

Believers must step over the line of reason and logic into the land of faith. The Bible declares that the just and the righteous, shall live by faith. Paul said, "I am not ashamed of the gospel because it is the power unto salvation for everybody that believes." That means everybody! Get bold for Jesus, step over the line, and break the huddle with timid, shy disciples.

God challenges each Christian who really loves Jesus to step over the line. If you're saved, step over the line. Every choir member should step over the line. Every deacon, trustee, usher, and church member needs to step over the line. The world needs us to show how bad we are for Jesus. When rap groups (saying that they represent today's culture) can degrade women by calling them that "B" word, it's time to step over the line.

It's time for the church to break the huddle of carnality and compromise to step over the line and show the world we're tough and we can stand

> IT'S TIME FOR THE CHURCH TO BREAK THE HUDDLE OF CARNALITY AND COMPROMISE TO STEP OVER THE LINE AND SHOW THE WORLD WE'RE TOUGH …

up for the gospel. When "PG" (parental guidance suggested) movies have more profanity in them than what you hear in military barracks, it's time for the Church to step over the line. It is time to step over the line and show this perverted world that we dare to be different! We dare to break the huddle with the status quo.

When abortion is accepted by Christians as an alternative in crisis pregnancy or for a convenient lifestyle solution, it is time to step over the line. When cartoon artists like "The Simpsons" contain verbal abuse and kids disrespecting their parents, it's time to step over the line. When violence and murder are at an all time high and the abundant life that Jesus brought us is at an all time low, it's time to break the huddle and step over the line of mediocrity … step over the line of being average.

Let the redeemed of the Lord say so. If you love Jesus, say "Yes" to His Word. Say "Yes" to His will and "Yes" to His way. You need to break the huddle of your comfort zone and show how bold you are for Jesus.

INTELLECTUAL SHAME

Christians need to break the huddle and step over the line, but we have a problem doing it. Why? Many Christians are literally ashamed of the gospel because we fear rejection, ridicule, and the potential loss of position or livelihood. Two reasons are at the root of this problem of being ashamed of the gospel. One is what I call, "intellectual shame." We fear that the gospel does not measure up intellectually. Today, you don't have to go to school and earn a degree to be an intellectual because of mass media. Regardless of whether you completed the first grade or you are a college graduate, television has given the world such access to information that most people have an intellectual mindset. If you're formally educated, you probably have a super-intellectual mindset. Regardless of our level of education, many Christians are afraid that the gospel does not measure up to self-imposed, intellectual standards of logic and reason.

> ... MANY CHRISTIANS ARE AFRAID THAT THE GOSPEL DOES NOT MEASURE UP TO SELF-IMPOSED, INTELLECTUAL STANDARDS OF LOGIC AND REASON.

It does not make intellectual sense that God made Himself incarnate. The first thing any intellectual will tell you is that God cannot make Himself. Jehovah's Witnesses emphasize the fact that God cannot make Himself. Intellectual arguments based on logic and reason can never prove or disprove a belief that is based on faith. By its very definition, faith cannot be proven as intellectually sound. Exercising faith requires believing in the substance of things hoped for, and the evidence of things not seen. Becoming a Christian means professing belief in something that can only be discerned spiritually. Ask the

Holy Spirit to help you discern truth from untruth as you grow up in Christ.

The acid test to determine whether someone is grounded in truth is the question, "What do you believe about Jesus?" In other words, who was He? Who *is* He?" If a person answers those questions by stating that Jesus is not Lord, then you know you're in a conversation with an unbeliever. In those cases, proceed with caution, lest you become confused yourself.

> WE NEED TO STEP OVER THE LINE OF OUR INTELLECTUAL MINDSET SO WE CAN BREAK THE HUDDLE AND SAY THAT WE ARE NOT ASHAMED OF THE GOSPEL!

Christians believe God is sovereign. God can do anything He wants to do, when He wants to do it, however He wants to do it. If God can make you, me, and everything else, why couldn't He make Himself? To people outside of Christ, it doesn't make sense that this great God would make Himself into human form, step down to earth, be tempted in every way, bleed, suffer, die a criminal's death, and on the third day be resurrected with all power in His hand. What kind of sense does that make for a Twentieth Century mindset? If we are very honest with ourselves and God, we will confess our intellectual shame, repent and step over the line into the land of faith.

First Corinthians 3:18-20 reads: "Let no man [or woman] deceive himself [or herself]. If any man [or woman] is among you that seemeth to be wise to the world, let him [or her] become a fool that he [or she] may be wise." We need to step over the line of our intellectual mindset so we can break the huddle and say that we are not ashamed of the gospel!

WE ARE INHIBITED
AS DISCIPLES BY
INTELLECTUAL SHAME
AS WELL AS
SOCIAL SHAME.

SOCIAL SHAME

A second reason causes us to be shy for Jesus, "social shame." We're scared that people are going to laugh at us or call us religious fanatics. It is easy to testify in the church! The majority of the people in the church know and love Jesus. But when you go to work Monday morning, many people you meet may not know Him. Someone may laugh at you or make fun of you when you stand up for Jesus. This is why many Christians go under cover between Sundays – we have an "under cover religion." We are inhibited as disciples by intellectual shame as well as social shame.

One time a church member let me know that she was leaving the church. I asked her: "Sister, why are you leaving?" She said, "I'm leaving because of what happened to me last Sunday. I was so happy I felt like I had to stand up. Something came over me but I can't act like that. I'm going to look for another church where I won't be tempted to act like that. I need to leave this church because I don't like what I'm becoming."

Many Christians are simply afraid to be free spiritually. We shouldn't fear what we are becoming in Christ because fear is not of God. In 2 Timothy 1:7-9, Paul says, "He has not given us a spirit of fear but of power and love and a sound mind." We find power and love in Jesus, and they make us free to believe based on faith alone.

TAKE A DECISION STEP

Let's explore three steps that will help you in stepping over the line. The first step is a "decision step." It is a step of choice.

> DECIDE TO HAVE
> A MONOGAMOUS
> RELATIONSHIP
> WITH HIM AND
> STEP OVER THE
> LINE TO SHOW
> THE WORLD THAT
> HE IS OUR
> ALL IN ALL.

Stepping over the line is a choice. Every time you wake up in the morning, you face a day of choosing between the flesh and the spirit. You cannot avoid dealing with your Mr. Carnal and Mr. Spiritual, or your Ms. Carnal and Ms. Spiritual. Every day means making "decision steps" regarding who you will listen to and follow. Every day you choose whom will you serve. You must make "decision steps" to effectively step over the line for Jesus.

You must decide to have one Love. Some people think being Christian means loving everything and everybody equally twenty-four hours a day, seven days a week. This may sound godly, but it isn't possible, nor preferable. Our love has to be built on a primary relationship with God first. Then we can love other people to a greater or lesser degree, depending on who they are to us in life.

Love for God is like love for your spouse. When I got married 36 years ago, my wife and I got straight on this issue from the beginning. We weren't going to have a relationship in which everyone else in our life had equal footing with us in our love for each other. We vowed to have a monogamous relationship with each other. In the family of God, we must have a monogamous relationship with Him where He comes first, your spouse is next, and mama and daddy and everyone else just have to take a number.

If you really love Jesus, God is calling for you to break the huddle every morning. Decide to have a monogamous relation-

> YOU MAKE A CHOICE TO LOVE GOD WITH ALL YOUR HEART, WITH ALL YOUR SOUL, WITH ALL YOUR MIGHT AND TO HAVE NO OTHER GOD BEFORE HIM.

ship with Him and step over the line to show the world that He is our all in all. Some of us want Him to be our Friend, but we don't want Him to be our Father. Some of us want Him as our Savior but we don't want Him as our Lord. Some of us want to call on Him every now and then, but we don't want to call on Him everyday. We want to be His friend but we don't want to be His lover. Some of us are trying to love God in the same way we love our friends. But God is saying, "Step over the line into a monogamous relationship with Me." Be bold! The first step is a decision step. You make a choice to love God with all your heart, with all your soul, with all your might and to have no other god before Him.

TAKE A DOGMATIC STEP

The second step is called the "dogmatic step." It is a sure step. This is the stand up for Jesus step. Some of us have come to the line but we haven't crossed over it. Some of us have our toe on the line, and in sports, that could be good or bad. In football, if the ball comes in contact with the line it's a touchdown, but in God's game plan, the rules are different.

In God's kingdom, we must step over the line. We can't be merely at the line. We can't just have our toe or foot on the line. We can't have just one foot over the line. We must fully step over.

Today the call is for every Christian to step all the way over the line. Break the huddle of procrastination and step all the way over! We need a dogmatic, absolute, sure stand for Jesus. Our forebearers used to say "If you don't stand up for something, you'll fall for anything." We cannot continue to be docile or passive, hiding in the crowd, or standing in the shadows. We cannot continue to be timid about our sanctification and cowardly about our Christianity. It is time to step over the line and show the world where we stand for Jesus.

When I first moved to Atlanta, it seemed like the city had more churches than any

> BELIEVERS MUST LEAVE THE BLEACHERS, GET ON THE FIELD AND STEP OVER THE LINE TO BE THE SALT OF THE EARTH AND THE LIGHT OF THE WORLD, A CITY SET ON A HILL

other place in the world. I said "This must be heaven!" I saw all kinds of churches: storefront churches, big impressive churches, urban and rural houses of God. I thought to myself, "Everybody must be saved in Atlanta with this many churches around!"

The problem is that too many of our churches are scared to call sin what it is – sin. Congregations and church boards have preachers scared to call sin sin. Churches desire to hear a message on love every Sunday but rebel against messages that deal with sin. Sin can do three things for you. It can take you farther than you want to go, keep you longer than you want to stay, and cost you more than you have to pay. Not calling sin sin keeps many Christians on this side of the line because stepping over might require greater holiness and sanctification in their life.

> MANY OF US ARE DETERMINED ABOUT OTHER GOALS, AND WE NEED TO BECOME EVEN MORE DETERMINED ABOUT JESUS.

As saints, we're called to be holy, to come out from under the covers and proclaim the goodness of God. Believers must leave the bleachers, get on the field and step over the line to be the salt of the earth and the light of the world, a city set on a hill.

THE STEP OF DETERMINATION

The third step and final step is called the step of determination. First, you make a decision to follow the Spirit; then you are dogmatic about it and take a sure step forward for Jesus. Finally, you become determined to step all the way over the line to show you're really "bad" for Jesus! In any situation worth a struggle, you must have determination.

When we feel like giving up, we need to go on. When we feel possessed by the devil's use of our intellectual mindset, we have to go on and step over the line by faith. When we feel possessed by the devil's use of social shame, we have to break the huddle, step over the line, and not be ashamed of the gospel before others. You have to be determined to make your stand for Jesus in modern-day society. Many of us are determined about other goals, and we need to become even more determined about Jesus.

> WE ALL HAVE OUR OWN INDIVIDUAL LINE DRAWN AT THE POINT OF FEAR WHICH IS MOST INTIMIDATING TO US.

> GOD WANTS US
> TO BREAK THE
> HUDDLE OF
> INTIMIDATION
> AND SHOW WHAT
> WE'RE MADE OF
> IN HIM!

MORE THAN CONQUERORS

We all have our own individual line drawn at the point of fear which is most intimidating to us. Are you under bondage to intellectual shame? Do you walk timidly because of the fear of social shame? Are you afraid you will fail because you don't have what it takes to step all the way over the line?

God tells us in Romans 8:38 that we are more than conquerors. Not just conquerors ... that's better than winning the Super Bowl! That's better than winning the World Series! God wants us to break the huddle of intimidation and show what we're made of in Him!

Don't worry. God's "got your back" as you cross over. The psalmist said, "Surely goodness and mercy shall follow me ..." (Psalm 23). Dare to be bold and see what happens. You really don't have anything to lose except worldly things, and if you happen to lose a worldly thing in being bold for God, He'll bless you with spiritual things so wonderful that words cannot do them justice. Be bold! Step over the line!

Chapter Seven
Review Questions

1. Use a dictionary to define the words "bold" and "timid."

2. Describe the childhood game "Step Over The Line." Why do children play games like this? How does this game relate to being an effective witness for Jesus?

3. What is intellectual shame? How does it hinder Christians from boldly stepping over the line?

4. Define social shame and the part it plays in causing believers to be timid witnesses.

5. Name three societal trends that ought to cause Christians to boldly step over the line for Jesus.

6. What is a decision to make a bold step over the line? How will it help you boldly step over the line?

7. Give the definition of a dogmatic step. How does this step relate to calling sin what it is – sin?

8. Fill in the blanks:

   When you take a step of determination, you step _____ _____ _____ _____ the line.

9. Name someone you know that has boldly stepped over the line for the gospel. What risks did that person take in stepping over the line?

FOR DEEPER STUDY

1. Read Hebrews 4:12-16. What reasons does this passage give to help us approach the throne of grace boldly?

2. Read Acts 6:7 - 7:60. How did Stephen boldly step over the line for the gospel of Jesus Christ? Can you image yourself being this bold?

HUDDLE GROUP DISCUSSION

1. Do you think the world considers the church "bad" enough to boldly step over the line for Jesus? Why or why not?

2. How has the church stepped back from the line by having a timid witness?

3. In what ways does the church have its toe on the line but has not yet crossed over it?

BREAK THE HUDDLE!

How have you avoided taking a stand for Jesus lately? Name one thing you will do that will show others that you are stepping over the line for the gospel of Jesus Christ.

BREAKING THE HUDDLE

Go a Little Further and Step a Little Higher
Matthew 26:36-39; Isaiah 6:1-8

> IN THE GARDEN, JESUS CLEARLY DEMONSTRATED THAT HE WAS FULLY MAN AND FULLY GOD.

FULLY MAN AND FULLY GOD

This message begins in the Garden of Gethsemane, Jesus' last stop before the cross. In Matthew 26:36-39, Jesus was in the Garden after the Last Supper, fully aware He was going to Calvary. In the Garden, Jesus clearly demonstrated that He was fully man and fully God. Just reading those words may not move you much; but it will rock your world if you really think about it. Jesus was fully man and fully God. Being fully man, He suffered everything that we might suffer, bore all our griefs, and knew all our temptations. God truly knows just how much we can bear.

In the Garden, Jesus as fully man, agonized over the will of His Father. He said to the Father, "If it be possible, take this cup from me." The Bible says His agony was so great that He sweat blood. Jesus, as fully God, as the Son, concluded the agony of

GOD MAY BE
CALLING YOU
TO YOUR OWN
GETHSEMANE.

the moment by surrendering to His Father's will saying, "Nevertheless, not my will, but Your will be done." Surely He was fully God; for what man would surrender to be crucified if he knew he had the power to stop it?

YOUR OWN GETHSEMANE

As we come to our own gardens of Gethsemane, we, like Jesus, agonize over the will of the Father. God may be calling you to your own Gethsemane. God may be calling you, and you are mentally sweating blood. It may be that you need to love someone that you don't want to love, someone that doesn't even love you, someone who may actually dislike you and mistreat you. As a Christian, a disciple of Jesus, you have a cup in your hand. You're supposed to love as Jesus loved, but you're praying, "Father, if possible, take this cup from me. I don't want to love this rascal! I don't want to love him!" Will you surrender to the Father as Jesus did, praying, "Nevertheless, not My will but Your will be done"?

WE ALL COME
TO POINTS IN
OUR LIVES WHEN
WE NEED TO MAKE
SPIRITUAL DECISIONS
LIKE JESUS.

We all come to points in our lives when we need to make spiritual decisions like Jesus did. We need to break the huddle and go a little further than we've gone before. I know in my life, I certainly have had decision points. The church has points of decision as well. When we come to decision points, individually and collectively we must be spiritually mature enough to pray, "Nevertheless, not my will, but Your will be done." Look to Jesus for strength because He can take you a little farther in surrendering to God's will.

> LOOK TO JESUS FOR STRENGTH BECAUSE HE CAN TAKE YOU A LITTLE FARTHER IN SURRENDERING TO GOD'S WILL.

JESUS WENT A LITTLE FURTHER

Before arriving in the Garden, Jesus and the disciples had taken of the cup and had broken bread together. Jesus as fully man must have felt extraordinary pain knowing His closest friends were about to abandon Him to the enemy. You will recall that the Garden of Gethsemane is where the kiss of betrayal and arrest took place. He took all of the disciples with Him. When he got to a certain point in the Garden, He told all but three to stay back. He took the inner circle with Him, Peter and the two sons of Zebedee. When He came to another point farther along, He told the three disciples, "You stay here and watch with me," because He had to go a little farther by Himself.

Those of us who have been washed in His blood and regenerated by His power must break the huddle with tradition and go further than the rest. All of us must go a little further. Break the huddle of carnality and try Jesus! As we contemplate our individual decision points, let us consider going a little further than we've been.

THE CHURCH NEEDS TO GO A LITTLE FURTHER

When we consider how we should feed hungry people and minister to the community, let us go a little further than we

> AS THE CHURCH
> EMBRACES HER ROLE
> IN ECONOMIC
> EMPOWERMENT
> FOR THE
> DISENFRANCHISED,
> LET US GO A
> LITTLE FURTHER ...

are right now. When we think of homeless people or ministering to the elderly, let us go a little further than others are willing to go. As the church embraces her role in economic empowerment for the disenfranchised, let us go a little further than we think we can. When churches face the decision point of expanding their Christian schools to cover kindergarten through grade twelve, let us go a little further than the community thinks we will go.

When we see all the children who live in violent neighborhoods exhibiting "at risk" behaviors, can we go a little further than the human services system? Can we strive for the assurance that Christian children will have a place to go to school where, at the very least, they will know *whose* they are and *who* they are? Can we help the children go a little further and get a vision for their life?

Somebody needs to teach African American children that they come from kings and that their history didn't begin on a slave ship! Somebody needs to teach all children that they belong to God, especially if they are homeless, don't know their parents, or are living in a foster home. All children need to know that they have a Father on high. Somebody needs to teach them that they are children of God.

Can we go a little further in our individual spiritual growth? Can we go a little further in our helping? Can we go a bit further in our tithes and in our offerings? Can we go just a little bit further in our praise? In Psalm 103 David says, "Bless the Lord, oh my soul and all that is within me." Do you have any praise stored inside that you need to release? I believe if you think about the goodness of Jesus and all that He has done for you, you will find a bottomless well of praise inside that you can draw from all the time. When you draw from the well of Jesus, you'll be glad to go a little further than you thought you could.

> IF WE COULD GO A LITTLE FURTHER IN OUR PRAYER LIFE, WE WOULD PLEASE GOD AND GROW SPIRITUALLY.

GO A LITTLE FURTHER IN PRAYER

One way to go further than you've been is to break the huddle of routine in your prayer life. It is interesting that many church members have not even once gone to a prayer meeting. I'm sure they pray in their homes, but every once in a while believers need to break the huddle of their cocoon at home to come and pray with the saints.

People will go to business meetings but won't go to prayer meeting. It's interesting how church members can go to board meetings but can't go to a prayer meeting? We can go to a council meeting but can't make it once to a prayer meeting. We might go to a workshop, a symposium, a public forum, or a political debate, but we can't find the time to come to a prayer meeting. We'll even go to a workshop on prayer! We willingly go to a symposium on prayer and pay a $40.00 registration fee, yet we won't break the huddle of being perpetual students and come to a prayer meeting. If we could go a little further in our prayer life, we would please God and grow spiritually.

GO WITH JESUS

Going a little further is a process. The *go* means to move along, to go somewhere new. Have you ever noticed that you cannot spell *gospel* without spelling *go*? Think about it! You cannot fulfill the gospel without going. "Further" means proceeding to a greater degree, which means that if you are here you must go forward to go there. It's also important for you to know who you're going with. You can't go a little further with just anyone. Young people shouldn't go to the prom with just anyone. Singles shouldn't go on a date with just anyone. A person shouldn't go to the marriage altar with just anyone. You always have to be concerned with whom you are going! When we break the huddle to walk the gospel walk, we must go a little farther with the Lord - not with other human beings. When you go with Jesus, you'll be on the right track because He is a mighty good Leader all the way from earth to heaven. Let Jesus lead you as you press on towards the mark of the high calling God has placed on your life.

> THE MAIN REASON MOST CHRISTIANS DON'T GO FURTHER THAN THEY'VE BEEN IS BECAUSE THEY THINK THEY'VE ALREADY ARRIVED.

The main reason most Christians don't go further than they've been is that they think they've already arrived. They think when they came down the aisle, gave their hand to the preacher, prayed a sinner's prayer and got saved, it was all over. Many church folks think they have it all and can't get any more. Many of us are sleeping on the gospel job. Jesus asked the disciples to stay awake and pray while He went a lit-

> YOU MAY HAVE A
> VISION FOR YOUR
> LIFE AS A
> CHRISTIAN, BUT
> IT WILL REMAIN JUST
> A VISION, UNTIL
> YOU PUT SOME
> ARMS AND LEGS
> IN MOTION TO GO
> A LITTLE FURTHER
> THAN YOU'VE BEEN.

tle farther, but they fell asleep. Satan is never too busy to rock the cradle of a sleeping saint. He just needs to catch you a little sleepy on your Sealy Posturepedic® mattress. He'll even make it soft for you. If you're dedicated to going further with Jesus, however, you'll stay awake on the gospel job. It's a 24-hour a day, seven day a week position with no vacation. Every day, you're expected to go further than you were yesterday. The cost of discipleship has always been high. Jesus paid the price so you can have the right to become a disciple, but you must pay the price of becoming a disciple. Nobody said the road to becoming more like Jesus would be easy. Lazy men and women aim low and usually achieve it. I don't believe He's brought us this far to aim low. Will you break the huddle of low aim and complacency to go a little further?

MISSIONARIES WITH "GET TO" ATTITUDES

Several factors exist that will catalyze going a little further than you've been – vision and passion. You must have a vision first. Then you must have the passion to see that vision come to fruition. Without vision, the people perish. Without passion, the vision perishes. Having vision without accompanying action makes you a visionary. Vision, with accompanying action, makes you a missionary. You may have a vision for your life as a Christian, but it will remain just a vision until you put some

> THE CHURCH
> NEEDS TO CHANGE
> ITS ATTITUDE
> FROM WHAT
> I CALL
> "GOT TO"
> TO
> "GET TO."

arms and legs in motion to go a little further than you've been. We can all go down in history as great visionaries but we must go a little further than we've been so far to be great missionaries. God called every church and every church member to be great missionaries. Will we accept the cup He has given us?

Does all this sound like a burden, an obligation, something you've "got to" do? If so, you may need an attitude check before going further. The church needs to change its attitude from what I call "got to" to "get to." What do I mean by that? We feel we've "got to go" to work but we "get to go" home. Some of us say we've "got to go" to Sunday School but we "get to go" to the ball game. We "get to go" fishing, we "get to go" play tennis, but we've "got to go" to a prayer meeting. Some of us say we've "got to go" to Bible study, but we "get to go" shopping. We need to change our attitude about growing the church from "got to" to "get to." We should say we "get to" go to church; we "get to" go to Sunday School; we "get to" tithe our money; we "get to" give an offering; we "get to" sing in the choir; we "get to" go to Bible study; we "get to" do God's will; we "get to" praise His holy name; we "get to" pray; we "get to" break the huddle and go a little further with Jesus.

We must change everything in our spiritual growth from "got to" to "get to." We need to realize that being a Christian is a privilege! We were bought with a price. We "get to" go just a little bit further like Jesus did in the Garden. It was His privilege to serve His Father by laying down His life for us.

A KING UZZIAH TESTIMONY

Sometimes it takes catalyzing events in our life to motivate us to go a little further than we have been so far. In Isaiah 6:1, Isaiah saw the Lord high and lifted up in the year that King Uzziah died. This is significant because King Uzziah had been Isaiah's friend, and we all go through something when we lose a friend to death. When King Uzziah died, Isaiah was moved to have a vision of the Lord where he was cleansed and received the call to "go" for God.

HAVE YOU EVER BEEN THROUGH A PAINFUL EXPERIENCE TO FIND THAT THE BLESSING IN YOUR SPIRITUAL GROWTH WAS GREATER THAN THE PAIN OF THE TRIAL?

I don't know what your King Uzziah testimony is, but in this scripture his death acted as a catalyst for Isaiah to experience the glory of the Lord. A time of trial led to a blessing! Have you ever been through a painful experience to find that the blessing in your spiritual growth was greater than the pain of the trial? In other words, when it was all over, the experience was worth it because of who you became in the process. Maybe you had an accident at some point in your life and that was your King Uzziah. You could've died, but the blood is still running warm in your veins today. When you think about it, does it cause you to go just a little bit further than you've been so far? Maybe the doctor told you that you didn't have long to live, but you're still fully alive today. Is your King Uzziah a deliverance from drugs or alcohol? Perhaps you thought you were going to be evicted because you had no money to pay the rent, but somehow a

> HAS GOD
> EVER SENT AN
> ANGEL WITH A
> COAL TO TOUCH
> YOUR TONGUE
> AND PURGE
> YOU OF YOUR
> INIQUITIES ... ?

check came in the mail! It's a King Uzziah experience if it catalyzed you to go a little further down the road of spiritual maturity.

Have you ever heard the cherubims singing "Holy, Holy, Holy?" Has God ever sent an angel with a coal to touch your tongue and purge you of your iniquities so that you cried out, "If the Lord needs somebody, here I am, send me! I'll go! I'll break the huddle! I'll go just a little bit further!"?

THE THREE-PART CALL

In Isaiah 6:1-8, Isaiah heard a three-part call. It was a "woe" call, a "lo" call and "go" call. The "woe" call was a word of confession. "Woe is me, I am undone." The "lo" call was a word of cleansing. A hot coal from the altar was laid on his tongue and his iniquity was taken away. The "go" call was a word of commission. God asked, "Whom shall I send? Who will go?" Isaiah answered "If the Lord needs somebody, here I am, send me."

Isaiah's vision was also three dimensional. He had an upward vision because he saw the Lord high and lifted up. He had an inward vision because he saw himself as undone. He had an outward vision because he saw the world in need, and he was willing to go further than he had been so far. "Here am I, send me." He had vision. He had passion. He was willing to act. He was a great missionary with a "get to" attitude.

Step Up a Little Higher as You Go

> Some of us need to get out of the slow lane and merge into the fast lane of commitment.

For the past two years, I have been involved with what is called "step aerobics." Step aerobics is an exercise routine that involves stepping up and down on a bench support with a certain number of steps, to lively music. It is designed to provide big muscle activity and increase heart rate and is good cardiovascular exercise. Those who are beginners just use the board supporting the steps, but they aren't ready to step up higher during the exercise routine. When you are stronger, you are able to step up and down on one step as you work out. Once you master one step, the teacher might allow you to move up to working on two steps because you're able to step up a little higher. When you have significantly improved your physical condition, you get the privilege to use all three steps and step up a lot higher than when you began. If you still want to go further and step a little higher, you can increase the tempo of the music and turn up the volume.

As we go along this gospel walk of ours, an analogy can be made with step aerobics and the church. Spiritually, some of us, and some of our churches, are still on step one. Some of us may be on step two, but we could step up a little higher. Many of us are ready for three steps, but we may need a King Uzziah experience to catalyze us to work harder so we can step up a little higher. Some of us need to get out of the slow lane and merge into the fast lane of commitment. The church

... IF WE WANT
TO GO A LITTLE
FURTHER, WE
HAVE TO BE
DISSATISFIED
WITH WHERE
WE ARE.

needs to increase the tempo, and pump up the volume. We will never "arrive" as Christians as long as we're on earth. We must strive to go further and step higher all along the Christian journey.

THREE SPIRITUAL TRUTHS

Three spiritual truths can guide us to go a little further and step a little higher. The first truth is that if we want to go a little further, we have to be dissatisfied with where we are. When we are dissatisfied, the Holy Ghost can do for us what He has been wanting to do for a long time. Some of us quench the Spirit because we are too satisfied with ourselves spiritually. We don't become disciples overnight! We grow in grace. When we receive the Holy Spirit, there is a filling; but just because we got some filling then doesn't mean we can't get more now. We can always step up just a little higher. We can always go a little further with the Lord than we've gone so far. Getting saved is complete; but it also is the beginning of a process. We are sealed to redemption, but that sealing marks the beginning of a process of spiritual growth that is ongoing. We must first become dissatisfied with our level of filling from the Holy Ghost to desire to be continuously filled.

... TO GO
A LITTLE FURTHER,
WE MAY HAVE
TO GO
BY OURSELVES.

> JESUS WENT
> A LITTLE FURTHER
> THAN ANYONE
> THOUGHT HE
> WOULD, AND
> STEPPED UP
> A LITTLE HIGHER
> THAN THOSE
> AROUND HIM.

A second truth is that to go a little further, we may have to go by ourselves. That is exactly what Jesus did! He told the three disciples to stay and pray, then Jesus went a little farther by Himself. We may have to go a little further than our spouse is willing to go. We may have to go a little further than the next church member. Leaders must go further than followers. Leaders, you must know the way, go the way, and show the way.

The third truth is that we must let Jesus be our Leader because He is a mighty good one. The Bible is full of good leaders who went just a little bit further. When Moses stepped up on Mount Sinai while the children of Israel were building a golden calf, he was stepping up higher than the others were able to do. When Abraham took little Isaac up on Mt. Moriah, he went a little further for the Lord than most fathers would. When Elijah stepped up on Mt. Carmel to go up against the 400 prophets of Baal, he stepped up a little higher.

JESUS IS OUR EXAMPLE

Jesus went a little further than anyone thought He would, and stepped up a little higher than those around Him. Jesus was sitting on the throne with the Father but He was willing to go just a little bit further. He broke the huddle with the Father, stepped out of eternity into time, and went a little further than He had been. Jesus went farther in the Garden of Gethsemane to the Mount of Olives, the oil press.

As He anguished, agonized, sweat blood and looked at the bitter cup, He prayed, "Father, if possible, take this cup from me." He didn't want to have to go to the cross. He wanted to stop right there. He didn't want to take another step. "If possible, take this cup from me." Somebody once asked me, "What did He see in the cup?" I think He saw my sins, your sins and all the sins of the world. He saw my soul and your soul burning in hell. He saw your

I'M GLAD JESUS HAS GONE FURTHER THAN ANYONE ELSE WOULD TO SAVE US FROM THE PENALTIES OF OUR FALLEN SINFUL NATURE.

head and my head under the heel of the devil. He saw my mama's soul, your daddy's soul; and our childrens' souls being tortured in the fire of hell. I'm so glad He was willing to go just a little bit further for me and you – aren't you?

Jesus, as fully man, stepped up a little higher. He stepped up higher to Golgotha's Hill; stepped up higher to Calvary. He bled, died and was buried; but He had to go just a little bit further than that! On the third day, Jesus, as fully God, stepped up out of the grave with all power in His hand and ascended into heaven to sit on the right hand of God the Father where He will judge the quick and the dead. He stepped up to the Mercy Seat, and is pleading my case and your case. I'm glad Jesus has gone further than anyone else would to save us from the penalties of our fallen sinful nature.

WILL YOU GO FURTHER AND STEP HIGHER?

Jesus is a mighty good Leader. Will you follow Him on the road to spiritual maturity? Where are you today in Christ, and

> ... DON'T BE AFRAID TO GO A LITTLE FURTHER ALONE BECAUSE YOU CAN'T WAIT ON ANY ONE ELSE.

how long have you been there? Have you been sleeping on the gospel job because you want to avoid the cup God has given you to drink? Do you need a King Uzziah experience to rock your world so you will want to go further than you've been? Are you out of shape because you haven't even started stepping at all?

If you have been blessed by feeling dissatisfied with your spiritual growth, don't be afraid to go a little further alone because you can't wait on any one else. Remember, God is always with you. We are all on this journey together, but we all need to break the huddle because each person walks alone with the Lord. Are you at a decision point in your life? Step up higher in faith and go further than you ever imagined you would for God. Begin now by praying, "Nevertheless, not my will, but your will be done."

CHAPTER EIGHT
STUDY GUIDE

1. Describe Jesus' experience as fully man in the Garden of Gethsemane.

2. How did Jesus demonstrate He was fully God in the Garden?

3. Meditate on your answers to questions one and two above. How does it make you feel to zoom in on Jesus' experience when He went a little further than all the rest in the Garden?

4. How does going a little further relate to decision points people face in their life?

5. Name five ways the whole church can go a little further in ministry.

6. Fill in the blanks:

   You can't go a little further with _____
   _____ .

We must go a little further with _____ _____ and not _____ .

7. List five areas where individuals could go a little further as growing Christians.

8. Why do many Christians tend to stay where they are rather than going a little further spiritually?

9. Describe how vision and passion catalyze us toward going a little further.

10. What is a "get to" attitude? How does it relate to going a little further?

11. How did King Uzziah's death catalyze Isaiah to go a little further with God?

12. Give examples of a Christian's growth using step aerobics to illustrate:

Using the board only:

One Step:

Two Steps:

Three Steps:

13. What are the three spiritual truths that guide us in the way to go a little further and step up a little higher?

FOR DEEPER STUDY

1. Read Acts 9:1-28. How did Saul go further than he ever imagined he would for God?

2. Read John 6:53-69. What decision point occurred that resulted in the twelve disciples going a little further with Jesus?

HUDDLE GROUP DISCUSSION

1. Name a ministry within your church that needs to go a little further. Why does it need to go further? Be specific about how it could advance.

2. Jesus went a little further for you. Are you sure you're born again in Him? How do you know you've gone far enough to really receive the free gift of salvation?

3. Describe someone you know who is using all three steps and a fast tempo in his or her spiritual aerobics skills as a witness for Jesus.

BREAK THE HUDDLE!

Name one area of your spiritual walk with Christ where you need to go a little further. What will you do to get in better shape and step up higher for Jesus?

BREAKING THE HUDDLE

Be Careful How You Build Your Ministry
1 Corinthians 3:9-15

> AMERICA HAS
> DEVELOPED ... A
> "HOME DEPOT"
> ORIENTATION ...
> WE LIKE TO
> FIX IT
> OURSELVES
> WHEN WE CAN.

GOD IS OUR MASTER BUILDER

In 1 Corinthians 3:9-15, Paul speaks to the church at Corinth, realizing that they were greatly influenced by Greek culture and their great philosophers such as Plato, Aristotle and Socrates. Small children learned philosophy at an early age in Greek culture like children in Hawaii learn to swim and surf at an early age. In addition to being great philosophers, the Greeks were also great architects and master builders. Athenian culture had poured over into Greece, which influenced the Greeks to become great builders of sculpture, palaces and castles. Many of their architectural masterpieces are still considered some of the most magnificent ever built. American culture is certainly not known for the same kind of architectural expertise, but many people have a general knowledge of building and building supplies.

GOD IS ALL-SUFFICIENT AND WE MUST ACKNOWLEDGE THAT TO BUILD OUR SPIRITUAL TEMPLE.

America has developed what I call a "Home Depot" orientation because we like to fix it ourselves when we can. The cost of having a plumber come out is so expensive that even I know how to change the inside of a toilet myself! When we go to Home Depot, we have an enormous number of choices in building supplies available to us. When we fix it ourselves, we want to be careful to select the right building supplies because we value our home and want to make a good profit when we sell it.

In this passage, God is speaking to us about spiritual building supplies for our spiritual temple. Paul knew he was speaking to the architectural experts of his day when he said, "By the grace of God, I am a master builder." He gives God all the glory for being a spiritual Master builder! God is all-sufficient and we must acknowledge that to build our spiritual temple.

God built the firm foundation of Jesus Christ in us. Paul takes no credit for the foundation because it is Jesus and Jesus only! However, he cautions the Corinthians to be careful how they build on it. Paul explained that several types of building materials were available - gold, precious stone, wood, hay or straw. His point about carefully building the foundation of Jesus Christ warns that the day of judgment will come when what you build will be tested. If it survives, you will receive a reward. If it does not survive, you will suffer loss, even though you will be saved as through a flaming fire. Break the huddle and build your ministry, but be careful how you build it!

EVERYONE WILL BE JUDGED

Every Christian's works will be judged. We need to clear up this misconception that Judgment Day is only for sinners. Saints and sinners alike will stand before one of the judgment thrones! Just because you're saved doesn't mean you aren't going to be judged. Those who never acknowledged Jesus Christ as Lord and Savior are destined for hell. The Bible says that all of us in the church will be judged on the Day of the Lord. If you build using materials like gold or precious stone that survive, you will get a reward. But if you build with hay, wood or stubble, it will burn up and you will suffer loss, even though you will still be saved from the flaming fire of hell for eternity.

For example, if you awake to find your house on fire at 3:00 a.m., you run out. As you look back, you see that everything you owned is lost. You are saved, but you have suffered loss. Your possessions are burned up; your mink coat is gone … your certificates of deposits are just ashes … all your fine furniture is up in smoke. Everything you had is gone, yet you are saved. How do you feel? You suffered a great loss!

Some might think, "it doesn't matter how I get to heaven. I'll just be glad to make it in." You will be glad to get in, but it will be awful to get into heaven with your nightgown on fire. If your pajama tail is on fire, as soon as you get into heaven you will have to sit down and put it out. You might just make it into heaven smelling the smoke of your own loss!

Paul says you already have a firm foundation, but you must be very careful how you build on it. If you build with the obedience of gold, then you will receive a reward. If you build with disobedience, however, you will suffer loss. When you build with disobedience, you are building with hay and stubble. Be careful how you build your spiritual temple! Be careful how you build God's building! Break the huddle, but be careful!

JUDGMENT DAY FOR THE SAINTS

What will happen at the judgement of the saints? In heaven, everyone will not have the same experience! Three "R's" are important to remember. One stands for Revealing, another stands for Reward and the third stands for Regrets. Some revealing is going to occur at the judgement in heaven. Everyone you think is going to be there is not going to be there. Some of the people you expect to see will not be there. Some of those who jumped the highest and shouted the loudest will be revealed as phony Christians on Judgement Day because they won't be there in glory with you. You'll be in heaven wondering what happened to those people who were always jumping and shouting loud. If you built your spiritual temple with the gold of integrity and precious stone of love, then you will get a crown with a star for each one you brought with you. I would like to have a crown with stars rather than to just get in with my pajamas on fire! I would like to bring something to the Lord because I would like to receive a reward.

> "FRIENDS DON'T LET FRIENDS DRIVE DRUNK." … FRIENDS DON'T LET FRIENDS GO TO HELL!

Some saints will experience regrets because the Bible teaches that in heaven we will have an awareness of those who went to hell. How sad it will be if we have built our life of witnessing with hay, not saying anything to anyone about Jesus. Even if we go to heaven, some of our loved ones may go to hell because we didn't share the gospel with them. You'll be filled with regret if you are saved, with the awareness that you let your husband, your wife, your child, your classmate, your friend or your co-worker go to hell. A well-known slogan says, "Friends don't let friends drive drunk." Likewise, friends don't let friends go to hell! You will be saved, but yet you will suffer loss when those you love are not with you because you didn't try to share the gospel with them. Are you building with gold and precious stone or with wood and straw?

> THE FIRST INDICATOR OF YOUR BUILDING SUPPLIES IS "ATTITUDE."

BUILDING SUPPLY INDICATORS

With modern technology, computers can be programmed to make digital flashers as an indicator of something. Pretend you have a digital computer reflector that indicates if you are building with gold or hay as you read this section.

The first indicator of your building supplies is "attitude." In 1 Corinthians 9:17, Paul says, "For if I do this thing willingly, I have a reward." Willingness is a good indicator of attitude. How many of you have ever asked your teenagers to do something like clean their room or cut the grass? Often they do it in obedience, but don't do it willingly! Some of them, "cop an attitude." How do you feel when this happens? When someone "cops an attitude," it makes us feel like just doing it ourselves.

Many adult Christians are obedient with an attitude. Sometimes we come to church out of duty. In other words, we are not coming willingly. Sometimes we praise God with an attitude. "Oh Lord, I'll do it, but I don't really want to. Here we go with that deliberate, sacrificial expressive praise stuff again. I guess I will just follow along for the ride." Some of us "cop an attitude" when we tithe. We do it because we are obedient, but we don't really want to do it. The Bible says God loves a cheerful giver so we must do it willingly if we want a reward later. If you

> THE SECOND
> INDICATOR OF YOUR
> BUILDING SUPPLIES IS
> "AUTHORITY."

are doing it with an attitude, you may get to heaven with your pajama tail on fire!

How's your digital flasher? Is it flashing gold or hay? What's your attitude toward your church? What's your attitude toward your pastor? What's your attitude toward the people in your church? What's your attitude toward serving in the ministries of your church? What's your attitude toward being involved in Sunday School? If you see "hay," it isn't too late to change your building supplies!

Now you have an opportunity to reflect and change, but the Day of Judgement is coming when the Great Reflector will reflect from the Judgement Seat. All of us will stand before the Judgement Seat and give an account of our works. Do you remember that television series, "This Is Your Life?" What if you hear a voice saying, "I am that choir member that missed my robe when you took it home. I am that Sunday School member whom you ignored for four weeks. This is your life!" It could happen to any of us if we don't take the opportunity to reflect and change.

> ONE MUST
> BUILD ACCORDING
> TO THE
> AUTHORITY OF
> THE LAW.
> WHOSE LAW?
> GOD'S LAW!

The second indicator of your building supplies is "authority." In 2 Timothy 2:5, we read, "And if a man also strives for masteries, yet he is not crowned except he strives lawfully." One must build according to the authority of the law. Whose law? God's law! Whose rules? God's rules! We all have to play by the rules. And although we may strive for mastery, we don't get a reward unless we do it lawfully.

Many of us have been athletes and can remember how some coaches give punishment in practice. I remember one punishment was to make us run laps around and around the outside boundaries of the athletic field. If the coach turned his head, some players would hide in the bushes or behind the bleachers. When everyone was going around the final time, they would run out from the bushes or bleachers as if they had been running all the time. If the coach caught them, which he sometimes did, he would just tell them to run extra laps for cheating. God doesn't tell you to run extra laps for cheating. He just says, "You're in. Yes, you're in – but no reward." There is no crown unless it's done lawfully according to the authority of the Scriptures, which is the Word of God.

> THE THIRD INDICATOR OF THE BUILDING MATERIALS BY WHICH YOUR WORK WILL BE JUDGED IS "ABILITY."

How is your digital flasher? Is it flashing gold or is it flashing hay? I'm afraid many Christians are trying to do their own thing, their own way, leaning on their own understanding and their own opinions. Saved? Yes. But there is no crown, no reward and your pajamas may be smoldering!

The third indicator of the building materials by which your work will be judged is "ability." Luke 12:48b says, "... for unto whomsoever much is given, of him shall be much required..." Ability is often referred to as the spiritual gifts and talents of the saints. Everyone has a spiritual gift, and some have more than

THE FINAL INDICATOR OF YOUR BUILDING MATERIALS AND CRITERIA BY WHICH EVERY PERSON'S WORKS WILL BE JUDGED IS "ASPIRATION."

others. Your gift can be a blessing or it can be a curse. It is a blessing if you use it for God. It is a curse if you don't use it for Him. You will receive a reward if you use it. You will regret it if you don't. What is your gift? Do you have an extraordinary voice but refuse to sing in the choir? Is your reflector flashing hay? Do you have the gift for accounting but don't want to help the church count, or create and monitor ministry budgets? Is your reflector flashing gold or hay? Do you have the gift of leadership? Do you have teaching ability? Are you using your abilities to glorify God willingly? What does your reflector say? The message for saints is be *careful* how you build your house! When you break the huddle, be *careful* how you build your ministry!

The final indicator of your building materials and criteria by which every person's works will be judged is "aspiration." The Scripture reference is 1 Kings 8:17-18. Aspiration deals with motivation – your desire and the reason behind your motives. First Kings 8:17-18 says, "And it was in the heart of David, my father, to build a house for the name of the Lord God of Israel. And the Lord said unto David, my father, whereas it was in thine heart to build a house unto my name, thou didst well that it was in thine heart." David wanted to do it for God, and so he got a reward. You have to be motivated to glorify God – not yourself. You have to want a closer walk with Him. You have to want God to give you a sanctified life. You have to want to

> GOD HAD
> THE FIRST
> HOME DEPOT
> OPERATION, AND
> HE GAVE US
> FREE WILL
> TO ROAM AROUND
> AND CHOOSE OUR
> BUILDING MATERIALS.

hunger for His Word. You have to want to praise Him when you don't feel like praising Him. You have to want it. You have to want to be obedient to His Word. You have to want to build your house with gold and precious stone. You have to have it in your heart! You have to want to be saved. You have to want to be sanctified. Outward obedience with ungodly motives on the inside gets no reward. How is your digital flashing? With gold or hay?

GET IN AND GET A REWARD

Be careful how you build your spiritual temple! Thank God we all start with the same firm foundation of Jesus. God had the first Home Depot operation, and He gave us free will to roam around and choose our building materials. I don't know about you, but I don't want to run this race in vain. Just getting in with my pajamas on fire is no reward.

Pray and ask Him: Dear God, help me build my house with a willing attitude and obedience that recognizes Your Word as my authority. Help me use my abilities to their greatest potential for all the right reasons, with a pure heart that loves You. Let my spiritual temple be built so that fire will reveal it to be built with gold. Bridle my tongue, hold my hand, keep my mind while I run this race because I don't want to run this race to suffer loss.

CHAPTER NINE
STUDY GUIDE

1. Why must you build carefully on the foundation of Jesus Christ? What are the consequences – positive and negative?

2. "You might just make it in smelling the smoke of your own loss." What does this mean? Describe this statement in your own words.

3. Define the three "R's" of the judgement.

4. Complete this sentence: "Friends don't let friends _____."

5. Which building supplies will survive the judgement? Identify a behavior for each category.

    Gold and Precious Stone –

    Hay and Straw –

6. Describe how attitude indicates the quality of your building supplies.

7. How does authority indicate the quality of your building supplies?

8. How will your work be judged according to the third indicator, ability?

9. What does aspiration have to do with the judgement of how you build on the firm foundation of Jesus Christ?

FOR DEEPER STUDY

1. For a greater understanding of ability, read Luke 12:42-48. What does this passage say about building well regardless of when the judgement will come?

2. Read 1 Corinthians 3:1-8. This passage precedes the foundational scripture for this message. How did Paul lead into the idea that we are master builders upon the foundation of Jesus Christ?

HUDDLE GROUP DISCUSSION

1. How is the church as a whole building unwisely on the foundation of Jesus with wood or hay? What are we doing that will not have a lasting effect on humankind?

2. Describe the ways the church as a whole is building with gold and precious stone? What ministry activities change society and make a lasting effect for generations to come?

BREAK THE HUDDLE!

For each indicator of building quality, identify one thing you will change so that your works will have a better chance of surviving when they are judged:

Attitude:

Authority:

Ability:

Aspiration:

BREAKING THE HUDDLE

10

A Prepared Soil for a Divine Harvest

Luke 24:48; Acts 1:8; Mark 4:3-20

> HISTORICALLY, EVANGELISM HAS BEEN THE RESPONSIBILITY OF THE PREACHER, THE MINISTER OF EVANGELISM, THE OUTREACH DIRECTOR, OR A HANDFUL OF SOUL WINNERS…

WORTHY TO BE SHARED

Christians don't hesitate to say that Jesus Christ is worthy to be praised! Given that – isn't He worthy to be shared also? When our hearts belong to Jesus, praise will naturally flow because we love Him and appreciate what He has done for us individually. True heart-felt praise is a personal thing, and each person has a unique way of expressing it. I love to praise Him as an individual, and I love to praise Him with others in the family of God. Sometimes I almost burst wide open with joy when in the midst of a congregation going from glory to glory in praise, song, and dance. What sweet experiences we can have together in praise! If He is worthy to be praised, however, it stands to reason that He is worthy to be shared.

IN ACTS 1:8
GOD SAYS,
"YE ARE MY
WITNESSES,"
WITH "YE"
MEANING ALL OF US.

I have prayed for an approach to evangelism that involves the whole congregation as effectively as praise and worship does. Can we find a way to share this gift from God so that anyone can use it easily? Historically, evangelism has been the responsibility of the preacher, the minister of evangelism, the outreach director, or a handful of soul winners, although God never said that spreading the gospel was the job of a select group of saints. In Acts 1:8 God says, "Ye are my witnesses," with "ye" meaning all of us. As a pastor, I have felt like a failure at times because of the limited number of people in the church who are eager to evangelize lost people in the world.

BREAK THE HUDDLE
AND SHARE JESUS
OUT OF THE
OVERFLOW OF HIS
GOODNESS IN
YOUR LIFE ...

A NON-THREATENING APPROACH

I have discovered an approach to sharing Jesus that is non-threatening both to believers and to those evangelized by them. It is non-threatening primarily because you don't have to memorize any Scriptures. As soon as people hear the word "evangelize," usually the first thing that happens is that they get scared because they think they're going to have to memorize something. You can share Jesus without intensive training. You don't need a method, and you can't do it "wrong" because there isn't just one way to do it. Break the huddle and simply share Jesus out of the overflow of His goodness in your life based upon your understanding of the nature of God, the nature of people, and your relationship with the Lord.

FOUR SEEDLING IDEAS

Let me share four seedling ideas that will grow this non-threatening approach to evangelism. The first seedling is that people need Jesus. Don't make it complicated because it isn't! People need Jesus.

The second seedling is that we are commanded by God to share Him. Luke 24:48 says, "Ye are my witnesses," but the word "witness" has several meanings. It can mean "to show" – and it's all right to show! You can be a witness by living a sermon before others, but that isn't what Jesus meant. He meant "tell," which is the Greek translation of "witness."

> THE FOURTH SEEDLING FOR … EVANGELISM IS THAT YOU MUST HAVE THE PRESENCE OF GOD IN YOUR OWN LIFE.

Paul was talking about "showing" when he said his life should be a letter or an epistle of the Lord. In Luke, however, Jesus is saying that we should be His "telling witnesses."

Third, you must have access to supernatural power. Natural humankind needs supernatural power, the Holy Spirit, to be an effective "telling witness." A car won't start if it doesn't have any power, but you can "jump" it by connecting the dead battery to a live one. A lot of churches today won't start because they need to be "jumped off." Some believers and churches are dead today because their battery has run dry. Many of us need a jump start from the Holy Spirit.

The fourth seedling for growing a non-threatening approach to evangelism is that you must have the presence of God in your own life. Very simply, you can't share what you don't have. It doesn't take a genius to figure that out! When I was growing up in Alabama, we had a ritual we called "halfus." When you bought something from the store like a candy bar, your buddies could call "halfus," and according to our subculture, you were required to give them half of it. So, if I bought a honey bun or a Moon Pie, as I walked out of the store I would call "no halfus!" Calling "no halfus" meant no one was entitled to call "halfus" because I had already beat them to it. The point here is that no one can call "halfus" on you for Jesus if you don't know Him. You can't share Jesus if you have no Jesus. Half of nothing is nothing.

> WHILE WE ARE COMMANDED TO BE HIS WITNESSES, WE ALSO HAVE A PROMISE THAT THE HOLY SPIRIT WILL BE WITH US.

While we are commanded to be His witnesses, we also have a promise that the Holy Spirit will be with us. Being "telling witnesses" is a big responsibility, but God will never leave us alone when we break the huddle for Him. In the Great Commission, God says, "Go ye..." and then says, "Lo, I will be with you..." Believers have the sweet assurance that the Holy Spirit precedes our witness. Whenever you sincerely "go" for Him, the Holy Spirit has already been there before you to prepare the way. All you have to do is go and trust that the Holy Spirit has done His job getting things ready for you to tell of His goodness.

A Parable for Heavenly Understanding

In Mark 4:3-20, Jesus gave us the parable of the sower to illuminate our spiritual walk with Him. Jesus used parables to teach because they are earthly stories that have heavenly meanings. God knew we needed simple, earthly illustrations to give us heavenly, spiritual understanding. In this particular para-

Break the huddle of conventional thought and realize that the church must be a sower and a prepared soil in order to reap an abundant harvest for the kingdom of God on earth.

ble, Jesus told about a sower who went along sowing seeds that fell into four kinds of soil. Sometimes, Jesus would leave the interpretation to the hearer. In this case, He went on to explain the meaning because its truth was too important to risk human misinterpretation. In this parable, the seed is the Word, and the soil is the world.

In the parable, the sower plants seeds that fall on four types of soil. Some seeds fall on the wayside, and the devourer comes and eats them up. Some seeds fall on stony places and spring up immediately, but because they are unable to develop an effective root system, they wither quickly in the hot sun. Some seeds fall on thorny soil that chokes the seedlings, not allowing them to grow to maturity. Finally, some seeds fall on good soil and grow well, bringing forth fruit in abundance.

Most people interpret the church to represent the sower, but we also represent the soil and it is very important that we be a

> **THE SEED IS ALWAYS GOOD! WE NEVER HAVE A SEED PROBLEM! WHEN PROBLEMS OCCUR, IT IS A SOIL PROBLEM.**

prepared soil. We are ambassadors for Christ, sowing seeds, but we also must be good soil for the seed Christ sows in us. Break the huddle of conventional thought and realize that the Church must be a sower and a prepared soil in order to reap an abundant harvest for the kingdom of God on earth.

It is important that the Church be a prepared soil to reap a divine harvest. The seed is always good! We never have a seed problem! When problems occur, it is a soil problem. The parable doesn't say bad seed fell anywhere. God does not produce bad seed.

> **THE CHURCH ... HAS BECOME POOR, UNPREPARED SOIL – A WAYSIDE – STONY GROUND AND A THORN PATCH FOR SPIRITUAL GROWTH.**

If you wonder why some churches don't grow, it isn't because they don't have strategies and methods. It is good to have plans and strategies, but ultimately, they are not the producers of church growth. Churches don't grow because they have a spiritual problem, no matter where they are located. Lack of growth is always a spiritual problem.

THE CHURCH HAS A SOIL PROBLEM

Mainline churches don't want to hear the news that lack of growth is a spiritual problem. So many churches are going around looking for methods, strategies, procedures, and techniques to enhance growth. Pastors and leaders are often in a huddle, bouncing from one conference to another, looking for the right church growth idea or program to solve their problem. The Church doesn't have a methodology or technique problem – we have a spiritual problem! We are not good soil! The church herself has become poor, unprepared soil – a wayside – stony ground and a thorn patch for spiritual growth.

When immorality exists in the church, nothing is going to grow there. Immorality in preachers, deacons, and members does exist, and the devil is having a field day with the leadership of the Church. The Church and her members have ungodly behavior and even tolerate sinful living from their leaders. Is it any wonder that the seedlings of eager evangelism are difficult to grow in the congregation's poor, unprepared soil? Is it any wonder that church growth leaders would rather stay huddled up in workshops and conferences rather than face the music that is playing on this issue?

> ALKA SELTZER® CHRISTIANS FIZZLE OUT QUICKLY BECAUSE THAT CHURCH IS NOT A SOIL PREPARED TO GROW THEM.

POOR SOIL INTO GOOD SOIL

Sometimes, our soil is poor because it is stony ground. On stony ground, the seed springs up, but quickly fizzles out. I call that "Alka Seltzer® Christianity." It has a fizz to it. Everybody gets happy on Sunday morning. People run down the aisle to join the church. As soon as they get there, they sign up for everything. They want to work on every committee. Two months later, however, you wonder where they are. Alka Seltzer® Christians fizzle out quickly because that church is not a soil prepared to grow

> WHEN SEEDS FALL ON THORNY GROUND, PEOPLE ARE MORE CONCERNED ABOUT WHAT THEY HAVE AND THE IMAGE OF WHERE THEY WORSHIP.

them. Since the love, mercy, and grace demonstrated in that church is so stony, their roots cannot go deep. As soon as trials or disappointments come, or if some one walks past them on Sunday and doesn't speak, they drop out.

A church can also be a field of thorny soil. I'm so glad God didn't leave the parable of the sower to our interpretation. He tells us that the thorns represent a lifestyle of materialism. When seeds fall on thorny ground, people are more concerned about what they have and the image of where they worship. They often worship the buildings more than they worship Jesus. The church as thorny soil is in bondage, and I know because I've been there and done that myself.

Years ago, I built a home in Shaker Heights, Ohio, and I loved it so much that I would sit in the living room looking out at the snow while playing Lou Rawls albums, thinking, "Now I have a piece of the pie!" Another source of pride was my 1973 Cadillac Eldorado. I would pull up in my driveway and just sit there for a while in pride. Back then, I wasn't good soil for the seed Christ wanted to sow in me. When I was materialistic, my spiritual life was choked out. That was then, but the danger of being thorny soil is very real for many Christians in the church, particularly successful Baby Boomers. The love of material things is such a strong huddle that you may not even realize you're in it.

The good news is that poor soil can become good soil when we let God plow us up and have His way with our field. We can grow spiritually, and the seedlings of eager evangelism will bear much fruit if we are willing to be His field. To grow and be "telling witnesses," we must both plow for and be plowed by the Lord. Often, the gospel falls on deaf ears because a church has not allowed itself to be properly plowed by God. Plowing comes before sowing, and we must be plowed ourselves before we can sow the seed in other people. Since we neglect being plowed ourselves, it comes as no surprise that we forget to plow first when we share Jesus with the world.

HOOKED UP TO THE POWER

How can Christians be plowed after they accept Christ? Once saved, you will be plowed as you mature if you remain hooked up to the Power that makes things grow. This power comes from the Holy Spirit, and it acts like the sun to bring the seedling up to its full fruition. To remain hooked up to the power of the Holy Spirit, the first thing you must do is confess your sins. God will not shine the Holy Spirit through the veil of unconfessed sin.

> TO REMAIN HOOKED UP TO THE POWER OF THE HOLY SPIRIT, THE FIRST THING YOU MUST DO IS CONFESS YOUR SINS.

Many of us use the excuse, "Well, we have all sinned and fallen short of the glory of God!" The issue is not about all – the issue is about you. God works with the individual. He wants the anointing on you. He wants you to be filled with the Holy Spirit. Confess your sins continuously and remain unveiled before the Lord so you can be hooked up to the Power that will fill you and plow you again and again. There is too much unconfessed sin in the church, and God isn't

WHEN YOU PRAY
IN FAITH, YOU
BEGIN TO ACT
LIKE WHAT YOU
PRAYED FOR HAS
ALREADY HAPPENED.

going to give the anointing necessary to evangelize until we have repented and confessed.

The second way to hook up to the power is by praising God in faith. You may have heard of praying in faith, but have you ever heard of praising Him in faith? Praise is hooked up to the Power when it is hooked up to His Word. Praise without God's Word is just plain partying – shouting, dancing singing, etc. Such praise becomes our party. Praise with God's Word makes it God's party. God's party generates available power.

Hebrews 13:15 says, "… let us offer the sacrifice of praise to God continually, that is, the fruit of our lips giving thanks to his name." If you ever come to church and don't feel like praising Him because of your situation or circumstances, hook up to Hebrews 13:15 and praise Him anyhow in obedience. When praise is connected to His Word rather than your feelings, you'll find yourself having a good time at the party you didn't want to go to, leaving with the power you need to share Jesus.

You also get hooked up to the power by praying in faith. When you pray in faith, you begin to act like what you prayed for has already happened. We have too much "casual prayer" going on in the church among believers. In many circumstances we don't know how to pray or what to pray for. We may spend a lot of time praying, but are we engaging in spiritual busywork, or are we really doing something meaningful with the right motives? For example, most of us spend more time praying for a saint who is getting ready to die and go to heaven than for sinners who are lost and on their way to hell.

We will eagerly pray for healing, but pray hesitantly to overcome sin or to win a lost soul. Not prioritizing praying in faith to overcome sin or win a lost soul is taking the power of prayer casually. Casual prayer is not strongly hooked up to the power, and so it doesn't plow

> WHEN YOU TELL SOMEONE ABOUT THE GOODNESS OF JESUS IN YOUR OWN LIFE, YOU PLOW A LITTLE.

you very much. Casual prayer creates perpetually cloudy conditions for growing the seedlings of eager evangelism. Praying in faith for the most important things hooks you up to the power of the Holy Spirit. Praying in faith helps you grow and helps others around you do the same. When you pray in faith for someone to accept Christ, you need to act like and treat them like they are already saved. We often relate to unsaved people differently than we do to saved people; that is walking by sight, not by faith.

DO A LITTLE PLOWING DAILY

Most people who come to know Christ didn't get saved the first time they heard about Christ; they needed plowing first. When you tell someone about the goodness of Jesus in your own life, you plow a little. When you simply talk about what being a Christian has done for you, the ground is broken in the one who hears you. Beginning by telling someone why they need Jesus is like throwing a seed down on the hard ground and expecting it to grow. Be a "telling witness" for Jesus in your

> WILL YOU CHOOSE
> TO BE GOOD SOIL,
> A PREPARED SOIL,
> FOR THE SEED
> GOD PLANTED
> IN YOU
> AT SALVATION?

neighborhood, with your friends, and at work. It doesn't matter whether or not they join your church – just plow a little. It takes time to fully prepare a field, so do a little cultivation, a little plowing, everyday.

Think back to the person who led you to Christ and all the ways you were plowed in preparation. Share Jesus! If you have Him in your life, then I know He's done something for you. If He's done something for you, then it will be easy to be a "telling witness!"

CHOOSE TO BE A PREPARED SOIL

One of the most liberating things about being a Christian is that we are free in Christ to choose our behavior. Will you choose to be good soil, a prepared soil, for the seed God planted in you at salvation? Will you choose to continually confess your sins, praise in faith, pray in faith, and nurture the seedlings of eager evangelism? People need Jesus. If you have Him in your life, let others call "halfus!" then share Him from the overflow of His goodness because you will always get more!

CHAPTER TEN
STUDY QUESTIONS

1. In Acts 1:8, to whom was Jesus talking? Does it apply to us today as Christians? Why or why not?

2. Use a dictionary to define "evangelize." Why does this activity intimidate many Christians?

3. You can simply share Jesus based on your understanding of:

   The _____ of God.

   The _____ of people.

   Your _____ with the Lord.

4. What is the difference between a showing witness and a telling witness?

5. Describe the four seedling ideas that will grow a non-threatening approach to evangelism.

6. What is someone doing if he or she calls "halfus" on you? Have you ever had someone want some of your Jesus? What did you do?

7. Identify the two roles of the church in Mark 4:3-20.

8. If a church isn't growing, is the problem with the seed or the soil? Explain your answer.

9. Why is stony ground in the church producing "Alka-Seltzer® Christians?"

10. What does thorny soil represent? How does it choke spiritual growth in believers?

11. How can poor soil become good soil?

12. Describe three ways to remain hooked up to the power that makes things grow.

FOR DEEPER STUDY

1. Read John 15:1-27. This passage uses another analogy of nature to describe spiritual growth. Describe yourself as a branch as you reflect on your growth since being born again.

2. In the church, some weeds seem to be growing better than the true Christians. Read Matthew 13:24-30 and explain God's plan for dealing with the weeds.

HUDDLE GROUP DISCUSSION

1. Is your church producing any "Alka Seltzer® Christians?" If so, what can you do to help them grow deeper roots?

2. Do you have any thorny areas in your church that are growing materialistic Christians? If so, is this a new or old problem? Can you think of ways to improve this soil problem?

3. Is your congregation hooked up to the power? How fervently and frequently do you corporately confess your sins, praise God in faith and pray in faith?

BREAK THE HUDDLE!

There is no one totally righteous – no not one! What is your unconfessed sin right now? Confess it! Repent today so you can be hooked up to the power that makes things grow.

Breaking the Huddle

Lift Up Your Eyes and Utilize the Keys to the Harvest
John 4:6-42; Mark 8:22-25

> IT'S POSSIBLE TO LOOK AND YET NOT SEE CLEARLY.

LOOKING, BUT NOT SEEING CLEARLY

The Bible, as God's revelation to us, holds the keys to life, and to life more abundantly. One such scripture is found in John 4:35. In this verse, Jesus says, "Say ye not there are four months and then cometh the harvest. Behold I say to you, lift up your eyes." Notice He said, "lift up your eyes" and not your head. It's possible to have your head lifted up without lifting up your eyes. It's possible to look and yet not see clearly. Some of us are looking, but we are not seeing clearly. If we are to break the huddle effectively, we must see clearly.

To illustrate, let me share a personal experience I had when I was living in Shaker Heights, Ohio some years ago. I wanted very much for my daddy to come and visit me, but my daddy is not the visiting type of daddy. I love him dearly, and I know he loves me the same way, but he is just not the kind of daddy that comes to visit. I have never even heard my daddy say, "I love you." I would like to hear that, even at this age, but he hasn't said it yet. When I told him I loved him, he became concerned about me. It seemed to scare him to death! Fathers from older generations generally don't deal in that kind of affectionate stuff, but I'm a huggy, touchy kind of person. I tell my sons all the time how much I love them.

However, when I was living in Ohio, I finally convinced him to come visit me. With great anticipation, I went to the airport to pick him up. At the same time, I had great apprehension because I was prepared for disappointment. Since I thought he might not show up, I got ready to deal with the potential disappointment. I went to the airport gate and watched intensely as people got off the plane, one by one. My daddy never came out! I went to the lady who was in charge of the gate, and I said, "Is there anybody else on the plane?" She said, "No." I said, "He's got to be on the plane!" She went and looked, but the plane was empty, and I prepared to go and drown in my sorrow. Suddenly from behind, somebody touched me on the shoulder. I turned around – it was my daddy holding a baby! He had helped a woman get off the plane with her child. He had seen me, but I hadn't seen him. He was wondering why I was standing up there looking crazy.

> MANY CHRISTIANS DON'T PARTICIPATE IN THE HARVEST BECAUSE THEY DON'T SEE THE HARVEST OR THE NEED FOR IT.

Why didn't I see him? My mind wasn't prepared to see him. My heart was not prepared to see him. My mind and my heart would not allow my eyes to see him. The old folks used to say it this way: "You see what you want to see and you hear what you want to hear." I would modify that a bit to say you see what you expect to see, and you hear what you expect to hear.

SEEING MEN AS TREES WALKING

Many Christians don't participate in the harvest because they don't see the harvest or the need for it. Jesus said in John 4:35, "Lift up your eyes and see…" Many see, but they don't see as they ought. Such was the case with the man from Bethsaida in Mark 8:21-25. Jesus touched him and asked, "What do you see?" The man replied, "I see men but they look like trees walking." He was not seeing clearly. He needed a second touch from Jesus.

MANY IN THE CHURCH HAVE RECEIVED THE FIRST TOUCH, BUT THEY NEED A SECOND.

When we go to work, many of us don't see souls that need to be saved. We just see people walking, and they look like trees. We go out into the highways and by-ways of life, but do we see

people, God's creation, that need to accept Jesus as their personal Savior? Are they like trees walking, or are they unsaved people who are going to burn in hell if they die in their sins without the Lord?

Many of us have relatives and friends who are unsaved, but we just look at them as relatives and friends. We don't see them in hell, in torture and destined for eternal damnation. We are not seeing as we ought to see. True Christians have all been touched the first time at salvation. Many in the church have received the first touch, but they need a second. The unfortunate fact is that many saved people are not seeing the people around them clearly. They might as well just be trees walking.

Three Spiritual Truths

We need to consider three spiritual truths that will help us see the lost people around us clearly. First, we must see the world with spiritual eyes if we are going to see the harvest of lost and unchurched people. Lost and unchurched people are everywhere we just have to open our spiritual eyes in order to see them.

> A CHURCH THAT DOES NOT SEEK THE LOST HAS LOST FOCUS BECAUSE IT IS NOT DOING WHAT JESUS COMMANDED US TO DO.

The second spiritual truth we must understand that evangelism is not an option for Christians. The Great Commission, Matthew 28:19-20, is a command, not an option.

Third, evangelism for followers of Christ should be an obsessive obligation. Do you know what it means to have an obsession? People say that I am obsessed with every member of Greenforest being a part of a Sunday School class – and they're right! I am not only obsessed, I am possessed as well! I am obsessed with Sunday School and possessed with the Holy Ghost. I think it is a good obsession, so I tell my congregation, "If you want me to sleep at night, go to Sunday School!" I am obsessed because I know small group Sunday School is the only way we can nurture and minister to one another effectively. Evangelism is not an option for us. Why? The Bible tells us that's what Jesus came for – to seek and save the lost. It is our job to do what Jesus did, right?

Many people who have accepted Christ in the past have been wounded in church situations, and have forsaken the fellowship. They don't go to church anymore, which makes them part of the unchurched population. It isn't an option for us, but rather it is an obsessive obligation to reach all of the unchurched.

Let me take this a step further. A church that does not seek the lost has lost focus because it is not doing what Jesus commanded us to do. We must look for the secrets to unlock the barriers that are holding us back. We must look for the keys, and I believe three keys exist to help us. Put on your 3-D glasses, uplift your spiritual antennae and receive the three simple keys to unlock the door that keeps us from seeing the harvest clearly.

> THE FIRST KEY IS THAT WE MUST ACTUALLY SEE THE INDIVIDUALS IN THE MASSES AROUND US.

SEE THE MASSES

The first key is that we must actually see the individuals in the masses around us. Jesus was able to see the individuals in the masses. In John 4:6-42, he met the Samaritan woman at Jacob's well and the first thing He did was to be friendly to her. The disciples had gone to town, and He was resting there at the well when the woman came up. He said to her, "Can I have a drink?" This is friendship evangelism at its best! He didn't say, "I am the Lord God Incarnate. I am Jesus!" He just said, "Can I have a drink of water?" She then began to question his motive. "How is it, she said, "that you would ask a Samaritan woman for a drink? How is that, considering you are a Jew, and Jews and Samaritans have nothing to do with each other?"

Jesus quickly moved from the physical to the spiritual and said, "If thou knewest the gift of God, and who it is that saith to thee 'Give me to drink;' thou wouldest have asked of him, and he would have given you living water."

Notice how Jesus moved quickly from the physical to the spiritual. Then the woman tried to divert Him and get back on the physical again. She observed, "But you don't even have a bucket to dip the water." The woman was looking, but she wasn't seeing. Then Jesus really got in her business. Jesus will get in your business quickly when He gets close enough to do it. He said, "You have had five husbands and the one you are with is not your husband," which meant she was "cohabitating" – she was "shacking up."

GOD KNOWS ALL ABOUT US

We need to remember that God knows all about us. God knows our sins, our weaknesses and our secret addictions; He is just waiting for us to come to Him. When Jesus got in the Samaritan woman's business, she began to reveal that she, too, knew a little more than it appeared initially. She said, "You must be a prophet. I have heard of the Messiah." She asked Him, "Are you greater than Jacob who gave us that well? Are you a prophet? Are you the Messiah, the one that we are expecting?" Jesus said, "I am he." The Bible says she dropped her water pot and ran into the city saying, "Come and see this man that knows all about me. Is He not the Christ?" The Bible says that many believed because of her testimony. Many others after that also believed because they sought out Jesus, and they saw Him for themselves. We must see the individuals in the masses like Jesus saw this woman. We must let them know that God already knows everything, and He desires to give them Living Water.

LIFT UP YOUR EYES

While the Samaritan woman went to town to give her testimony, the disciples came back from town and found Jesus. He said to them, "Lift up your eyes and see the field." Why did He say, "Lift up your eyes?" I believe it was because they had been to town, but they hadn't seen the individuals in the masses, and they hadn't told anyone about Jesus! The woman dropped her water pot and went to town with a testimony, and the masses came running, looking for Him.

The disciples were simply standing with Jesus, but Jesus said, "Lift up your eyes," because they had been to town and hadn't told anyone about the gospel. They hadn't seen the masses because they were too preoccupied with their physical needs.

Then they wanted to divert Jesus from the subject by asking each other, "Did anybody get Jesus anything to eat?" Jesus answered them with, "My meat is to do My Father's will." You can go all day without eating and not be hungry when you're doing the work of the Father. Jesus meant it when He said, "My meat is to do My Father's will." The disciples had been to town and hadn't told anyone about Jesus because they

WE ARE ALSO PREOCCUPIED WITH BEING JUDGMENTAL.

were so preoccupied with their own hunger. They hadn't seen the individuals in the masses that day! Jesus wanted them to lift up their eyes and begin seeing the big picture.

PREOCCUPATION HINDERS SEEING CLEARLY

In addition to being focused on their stomach, the disciples were also preoccupied with their prejudices. Too many Samaritans lived in that town! We have a problem with that, too, We don't want to invite anyone to church who doesn't look like us, talk like us, or act like us. We make excuses saying, "They don't want to be with us anyway." God didn't ask us what they wanted! God told us to find them and bring them in.

We are also preoccupied with being judgmental. Many believers would have judged this woman. "We really don't want someone like that in our church." We would probably reject anyone who has had five husbands and is shacking up with number six. We would have seen her in her badness, but Jesus saw her in her sadness. She was sad because she had been seeking love in all the wrong places. She had gone through six men looking for fulfillment! We would have seen her in her spiritual immorality, but Jesus saw her in her spiritual emptiness. She was void and empty, and she needed the Lord. We're too hung up and preoccupied with the fact that people don't act like us or look like us. We want them to get cleaned up somewhere else first before we accept them. One of the keys to the harvest is to make sure that we see the individuals in the masses and extend the love of Christ to them.

> THE SECOND KEY IS THAT WHEN WE LIFT UP OUR EYES AND SEE THE INDIVIDUALS IN THE MASSES, WE MUST SEIZE THE MOMENT.

SEIZE THE MOMENT

The second key is that when we lift up our eyes and see the individuals in the masses, we must seize the moment. Jesus said, "Say not ye, There are four months, and then cometh harvest? behold, I say unto you, Lift up your eyes, and look on the fields; for they are white already to harvest." Some of us think we need to wait. The harvest is ready! We must seize the moment.

In farming, you know that any harvest goes through three stages. The first stage is green, the second is ripe and the third is rotten. If you observe a banana, you'll see it move through those stages quickly! When you get it at the store, it's green and you

THE THIRD KEY
IS THAT WE
MUST SHARE
THE GOSPEL BY
TELLING PEOPLE
ABOUT IT.

can hardly eat it. Take it home and in a day or two, it gets ripe. Wait three or four days, and its rotten, and the only thing you can do is throw it away.

Jesus meant, "Lift up your eyes. You say four more months and you'll start doing some harvesting. Lift up your eyes and see them coming. Look at them right now – the harvest is right now." We procrastinate by trying to figure it all out. We do too much analyzing, evaluating, planning, organizing, and criticizing. We suffer from a paralysis of analysis. Just do it! Tell somebody about Jesus today! We must seize the moment. Break the huddle and seize the moment!

LET YOUR WORDS SAY SO

The third key is that we must share the gospel by telling people about it. The Scripture says that many Samaritans of the city believed on Him from the sayings of the woman. The emphasis is on sayings. Many others believed because of Jesus' own words. Put the emphasis on words and sayings. Sooner or later, when you do effective evangelism, you have to use words. You have to be able to tell somebody what God has done for you. You have to be able to tell somebody about your relationship with Jesus. You have to be able to tell somebody about your experience with God. See the individuals in the masses, seize the moment, and share the gospel verbally.

The problem is that many Christians think we can evangelize effectively without words. Many believers think they can effectively lead someone to Christ without talking about Jesus and

> IT WOULD BE THE HEIGHT OF CONCEIT TO THINK MY LIFE COULD EVER BE GOOD ENOUGH TO REPRESENT WHO GOD IS AND WHAT HE HAS DONE FOR ME.

what He has done for them or about what the Bible says. Many people say, "I live by faith" or, "I'll let my life speak for me." That's a crutch. You should let your life speak for you, but you cannot do effective evangelism just by letting your life speak. I cannot live a good enough life to tell a person of Jesus' anointing death and resurrection without speaking. I cannot live my life well enough to be an example of Jesus' substitutionary death on the cross for my sins. That puts too much emphasis on me and not enough emphasis on Him. It would be the height of conceit to think my life could ever be good enough to represent who God is and what He has done for me. How conceited can you get to think that your life alone can be good enough to communicate the majesty of God and what Jesus has done? To evangelize lost and unchurched people effectively, we need to speak the truth to them as well as live it before them. Break the huddle and run "word plays." Break the huddle and don't be silent.

Many believed because of the Samaritan woman' testimony. She didn't just run back to the village and say, "I am going to let my life speak for me." She ran back and said, "Come, see this man and what he has done for me!" Jesus Himself didn't just sit there looking holier-than-thou. The Bible says many believed because they heard Jesus' words for themselves. Both human and divine words are what brought these people to know God. Effective evangelism must have words. Tell somebody about

Jesus and share the biblical truth of the saving power of Christ.

GOD HAS ALREADY PREPARED THE WAY

I want to offer some additional spiritual truths relative to lifting your eyes and utilizing the keys to the harvest. The Lord of the harvest is with us, goes before us and comes after us. Immanuel, means "God with us."Not only is the Lord of the

> NOT ONLY IS THE LORD OF THE HARVEST WITH US, HE GOES BEFORE US, AND HE COMES AND CLEANS UP AFTER US.

harvest with us, He goes before us, and He comes and cleans up after us. In other words, when you go tell somebody about Jesus, God has already been there. He has already plowed some ground. He has already worked on that heart, even though you don't know how He did it. He may have done it by giving someone a good job. He may have already done it by dealing with a person who lost a job. He may have done it through an illness or death in the family. He may have done it with a thorn in someone's side.

God has already worked on them before we come and give our testimony; but God isn't through yet. He is also going to come behind and clean up when we're done. You may water, and you may plant, but it is God that gives the increase. Any good work God starts, He brings to fruition, even if it is at the day of glory.

YOU OUGHT TO SAY SO!

If the Lord of the harvest has touched your life, you ought to say so. If God has been good to you, you ought to say so.

If God has saved your soul, you ought to say so. If God has made you whole, you ought to say so. James Brown tried to say articulate the feeling when he said, "Say it loud, I'm Black and I'm proud." James could've said it better. He seemed to know who he was, but he didn't know whose he was. He should have said, "Say it loud, I'm saved and I'm proud." We

> IF YOU ARE NOT SEEING WELL, THE LORD OF THE HARVEST IS AVAILABLE TO GIVE YOU A SECOND TOUCH.

should be saying, "Say it loud, I am working in the church and I'm proud." … "Say it loud, I'm tithing my money and I'm proud."…"Say it loud, I'm serving on the usher board; I'm singing in the choir; I'm a child of God and I am not ashamed of the gospel." Say it, and say it loud, "I am proud that I'm saved by the grace of God." If you know the Lord, you ought to say so. As Dr. Issac Watts wrote so eloquently in "We're Marching to Zion":

> Let those refuse to sing, who never knew our God;
> But children of the heavenly king,
> But children of the heavenly king,
> May speak their joys abroad,
> May speak their joys abroad."

GET A SECOND TOUCH!

If you are not seeing well, the Lord of the harvest is available to give you a second touch. You may be going to work everyday, but you're are not seeing clearly. You look at people but see them as trees walking.

When the Lord of the harvest took the blind man from Bethsaida out on the outskirts of town, and touched him one time, He asked the man what he could see. The man answered, "I see men that look like trees walking." Jesus said "You are not seeing as you ought to see." Then Jesus touched him a second time, and the man was able to see clearly. That same God is available to touch your life now. You may be saved, you may have been in the church all your life, but you aren't seeing the people around you clearly.

> LIFT UP YOUR EYES AND SEE THE INDIVIDUALS IN THE MASSES! LIFT UP YOUR EYES AND SEIZE THE MOMENT! LIFT UP YOUR EYES AND SHARE THE GOSPEL WITH YOUR TESTIMONY!

Lift up your eyes and see the individuals in the masses! Lift up your eyes and seize the moment! Lift up your eyes and share the gospel with your testimony! When you get a first touch, you may be able to talk about Jesus in the church. When you get a second touch, you can talk about Him on the job. When you receive the first touch, you can come into the sanctuary and praise Him. When you get a second touch, you can praise Him in the workplace. When you get the first touch, you can witness to your neighbor. When you get the second touch, you can witness to everybody. When you get the second touch, even the engine of your car will seem to hum, "Oh, how I love Jesus!" When you fry your bacon, it will seem to hum, "Amazing Grace." When you get a second touch, something gets on the inside of you and has to get out. When you see someone you'll say, "I know the Lord! Let me tell you what He's done for me! He has taken my feet out of the miry clay! He has given me a new start!"

> Do you need
> a second touch?
> If so, ask the
> Lord of the
> harvest to touch
> you again ...

Everyday is a New Beginning in Christ

Do you see unsaved, unchurched and hurting people around as trees walking? Would you like to be like Jesus? You can do it right now! The greatest thing about being a Christian is that everyday can be a new beginning because we have free will. We can choose how we approach life with the mind of Christ.

Will you lift up your eyes to see the individuals in the masses all around you clearly? Are you willing to seize the moment and avoid the preoccupations of the carnal being within you? Do you need a second touch? If so, ask the Lord of the harvest to touch you again so you can utilize the keys to the harvest. He wants to touch you again. He is just waiting for you to ask Him to do it!

CHAPTER ELEVEN
STUDY GUIDE

1. Explain how you might see, but not see clearly. Use a personal example if you can.

2. Fill in the blanks:

   (a) You see what you _____ to see.

   (b) You hear what you _____ to hear.

3. How do we see people as trees walking everyday around us?

4. What is the first key to seeing clearly? How did Jesus demonstrate this first key in John 4:6-42?

5. What sorts of preoccupations hinder us from lifting our spiritual eyes and seeing clearly?

6. Describe the second key to the harvest which helps us see clearly.

7. Fill in the blanks:

   (a) We do too much _____ , _____ , _____ , _____ and _____ .

   (b) We suffer from a _____ of _____ .

   (c) Just _____ it!

8. The third key emphasizes the importance of telling people about what Jesus has done for us. Is it possible to effectively evangelize without communicating? Explain your answer.

9. List the three spiritual truths that further illustrate how we can lift our eyes and utilize the keys to the harvest.

10. Compare and contrast three examples of the spiritual growth that occur between Jesus' first touch and His second touch.

FOR DEEPER STUDY

1. Read I Corinthians 13:9-12. What does this passage mean to you personally? In what ways do you yearn to see more clearly?

2. Read Matthew 9:35-38. What was Jesus' reaction when He saw the multitudes? Does the church really lift up her eyes and see like Jesus? Do we react to the multitudes with His heart or with our own?

HUDDLE GROUP DISCUSSION

1. In what ways does the church today suffer from a paralysis of analysis?

2. What kinds of preoccupations hinder specific ministries from being more effective? What can be done about it?

3. How can the church do a better job of helping members want to get that second touch from Jesus?

Break the Huddle!

Examine how effectively you are witnessing at home, at work or in your community. Pray that Jesus will touch you again so you will see more clearly how to utilize the keys to the harvest in your life.

BREAKING THE HUDDLE

Don't Let the Harvest Pass You By

Jeremiah 8:20-22; John 4:35-38;
Revelation 14:14-20; Matthew 9:35-38

> ... THE WORD
> IS LIKE A
> DOUBLE-EDGED
> SWORD.

THE WORD CUTS TWO WAYS

It is an awesome responsibility to learn and apply the Word of God because it cuts two ways. It would be nice if it only cut one way, but the Word is like a double-edged sword. It cuts one way to comfort and another way to disturb.

Three selections from the Bible demonstrate the urgency and importance of breaking the huddle and getting busy doing His will while we still have time to do so.

First, in Jeremiah 8:20-22, the recorder writes: "The harvest is passed, the summer is ended and we are not saved. Is there no balm in Gilead? Is there no physician there? Why then is not the health of the daughter of my people recovered?"

Second, in John 4:35-38, Jesus tells the disciples, "Say not ye, There are yet four months, and then cometh harvest? Behold, I say unto you, Lift up your eyes, and look on the fields; for they are white already to harvest. And he that reapeth receiveth

> ALTHOUGH THERE IS A HARVEST NOW; THERE WILL ALSO BE A HARVEST AT THE END TIME AS WELL.

wages, and gathereth fruit unto life eternal, that both he that soweth and he that reapeth may rejoice together. And here is that saying true, One soweth, and another reapeth. I sent you to reap that on which ye bestowed no labor; other men labored, and ye are entered into their labors."

Finally, in the book of Revelation, we thank God that He gives us a foretaste of the consummation of time, showing us how this whole thing is going to end. Although there is a harvest now; there will also be a harvest at the end time as well.

In Revelation 14:14-20, John, from the Isle of Patmos, described what God showed him in vision after vision:

> "And I looked, and behold a white cloud, and upon the cloud one sat like unto the Son of man, having on his head a golden crown, and in his hand a sharp sickle. And another angel came out of the temple, crying with a loud voice to him that sat on the cloud, Thrust in thy sickle, and reap: for the time is come for thee to reap; for the harvest of the earth is ripe. And he that sat on the cloud thrust in his sickle on the earth; and the earth was reaped. And another angel came out of the temple which is in heaven, he also having a sharp sickle. And another angel came out from the altar, which had power over fire; and cried with a loud cry to him that had the sharp sickle, saying, Thrust in thy sharp sickle, and gather the clusters of the vine of the earth; for her grapes are fully ripe.

And the angel thrust in his sickle into the earth, and gathered the vine of the earth, and cast it into the great winepress of the wrath of God. And the winepress was trodden without the city, and blood came out of the winepress, even unto the horse bridles, by the space of a thousand and six hundred furlongs."

These Scriptures are the foundation of this message about breaking the huddle and participating in the harvest while you still have time! Let me share an experience from my youth that illustrates how a fraction of a second can cause us, and others, to miss out on great things. You may have a story similar to this.

TOO LITTLE, TOO LATE

In 1954 the high school team I played on was in the regional final game, having hopes of winning and going on to the state tournament. We were up against a team that we had already beaten three times in edge-of-your-seat, one point victories. Now, we were meeting this same team again in the regional finals to determine who was going to the state tournament. As the game proceeded, one- and two-point leads changed hands over and over again until the final seconds of the game. With just a few seconds left on the clock, we were behind one point with the ball in our possession. The ball was shot towards our basket, and I positioned myself for the rebound. I jumped and attempted to tap the ball in. I controlled the board as I had often done, but this time the ball would not go in the basket. Each time it rolled around and off the rim, I would tap it again.

As I dreamed about this for years after, it seems I must have tapped it five or six times, over and over again. (In those days, there was no such thing as offensive goal tending as it is now. Players were able to control the ball above the rim.) I tapped it, and I tapped it, and I tapped it!. The clock went off – boom! Then the ball went in. The referee signaled "no good" because it was it was too little, too late.

BIBLICAL EXAMPLES OF TOO LITTLE, TOO LATE

The Bible is filled with many illustrations of too little too late. Think about the parable of the talents, and the one who buried his talent. When the Lord came back, the servant really thought he had done something good! When he found out he had made a mistake, he wished he could have made amends, but it was too little and too late. The Lord took his talent and gave it to another wiser steward. In the parable of the ten virgins, five went off to get some oil, but when they came back and knocked on the door, no one would let them in. It was an incident of having too little oil and getting back too late.

> JUDAS TRIED TO GIVE BACK THE THIRTY PIECES OF MONEY HE RECEIVED FOR BETRAYING OUR LORD AND SAVIOR, BUT IT WAS TOO LITTLE, TOO LATE.

Judas tried to give back the thirty pieces of money he received for betraying our Lord and Savior, but it was too little, too late. We find another illustration in the parable about the division of the goats from the sheep. When the goats were on the left and the sheep were on the right, the goats wished they could have made amends. They wished they could have changed in time to have been selected as sheep, but Jesus said to the goats on the left, "Depart from me." It was too little and too late.

DON'T LET THE HARVEST PASS YOU BY

The challenge in this message is: Don't let the harvest pass you by. Don't be guilty of doing too little, and doing it too late as well. Although the metaphor of a "harvest" seems agricultural, we aren't talking about wheat or tares, corn or grapes. What we are really talking about is the soul. Our task as disciples is harvesting souls for the kingdom of God.

> WE ARE HIS HARVEST, AND WE ARE ALSO CALLED TO DO HARVESTING WITH HIM.

As He prepared to leave Galilee, Jesus looked back and said to the disciples, "Look! The field is ripe; the corn is white and ready to harvest!" He saw lost souls who were ready to come to the light, ready to be in the kingdom. All of us are included in God's harvest. God is the Lord of the harvest, and as His workmanship, we are partners with Him in the harvest. We are His harvest, and we are also called to do harvesting with Him. We are both vessels and instruments.

Again, the challenge for us is not to let the harvest pass us by! Let us not be guilty of allowing the harvest to happen without us! We must participate in the harvest while we have time. Let us not be guilty of having too little faith, too little knowledge, too little commitment, too little giving, and too little service in our Christian walk. Break the huddle before you find out that you've done too little and been too late!

Our Scripture from the book of Jeremiah describes days of exile. The children of Israel had been marched out of their homeland of Judah and the city of Jerusalem. They were marched into the northern country of Babylon because of their

> BALM CANNOT BE
> FOUND IN A
> HUMAN BEING,
> NO MATTER WHAT
> TITLE THAT
> PERSON HOLDS.

iniquities. They sat there by the river Chebar, trying to figure the whole thing out. Harvest time traditionally was the latter part of March through May. "How is it that this time has gone?" they asked. Not only had the harvest time gone, but June, July and August had passed, the summer had ended, and yet, they were not saved.

Some people are asking the same questions today. Is there no hope? How long must I stay in this position? Is there no physician in the land? Have I missed something?

LOOKING FOR BALM IN ALL THE WRONG PLACES

The problem is that we, like they, have too often looked for the Balm of Gilead in the wrong places. There is only one Great Physician, and that is Jesus Christ. The problem is that we look for physicians in human beings. As we visit from church to church, some of us feel that the revelation is in a certain bishop or a certain reverend. Balm cannot be found in a human being, no matter what title that person holds. The Revelation is found only in Jesus Christ.

Some look for balm in prayer cloths that are probably made somewhere in south Georgia, and water that probably comes from some source like the Chattahoochee River. However, balm cannot be found in a prayer cloth. It is not in any water, from the Chattahoochee River or anywhere else. The Revelation, the balm, is in Jesus and Jesus alone. Some are looking for it in crack cocaine, in the bottom of a bottle, or somewhere else, but the Revelation, the balm, the Physician is found in Jesus and Jesus alone.

EVERLASTING CONSEQUENCES

Don't let the harvest pass you by! Don't be guilty of doing too little or being too late because the consequences are irreversible. John tells us of those consequences when he speaks to us in the fourteenth chapter of the book of Revelation. He tells us what God told him to write. God Almighty said "John, write this. Write it for all time. Write it for the people in America. Write it for the universe. Write it for My people so they might get a glimpse of how, and what it is going to be like." The Scripture tells us there will be a general harvesting of two groups at the consummation of time.

> DON'T BE GUILTY OF DOING TOO LITTLE OR BEING TOO LATE BECAUSE THE CONSEQUENCES ARE IRREVERSIBLE.

John says that he saw coming out of the heavens one who was like the Son of Man, who had a gold crown upon His head and a sickle in His hand. This sickle was cutting a harvest of those that would be in the garden of God. It was the sickle of mercy, grace and love, but he said it didn't stop there.

He said he saw another angel to whom God had given charge over the sickle of wrath, which was just as sharp as the sickle of mercy. This sickle of wrath and judgment cut through the grapes, and they were mashed and pressed through the winepress outside the city. The winepress didn't produce wine, it produced blood! Not a little blood but a lot of blood. Not the blood of the Lamb, but the blood of the slaughter.

> WE TEND TO
> PUT OFF WHAT
> WE OUGHT TO
> DO FOR GOD.

I don't know about you, but I want to be washed in the blood of the Lamb, I don't want to drown in the blood of the slaughter. The blood of the slaughter was so great that it was as high as the bridle of a horse, and it poured out for 200 miles. That's a tremendous amount of blood! I don't want to be guilty of doing too little and being too late so that I drown in the blood of the slaughter. I am not going to take any chances. I'd rather do too much and be too soon, than to do too little and be too late.

DON'T PROCRASTINATE

A second problem our text suggests is procrastination. We like to put things off. I'm not talking about secular procrastination, I'm talking about spiritual procrastination. We tend to put off what we ought to do for God. We put it off today and plan to do it another day, like procrastinating about enrolling in Bible study. We put off tithing and making commitments. Someone reading this now has decided to put off something for God until a better time comes. We put it in our minds, but we put off demonstrating it in our behavior. Some have been putting off a commitment to sing in the choir while many put off a commitment to do God's work in other ways.

The Bible says this is serious spiritual business! Jesus told the disciples to lift up their eyes and lift up their heads. Look to the hills from whence cometh your help! Look up and you will see that the harvest is plentiful but the laborers are few. Perhaps you are guilty of looking down or looking all around. Jesus didn't say

> ALL OF US
> HAVE A SEED
> SOWN IN US BY
> THE GREAT SOWER.
> THE QUESTION
> IS – WILL YOU
> ALLOW IT
> TO GERMINATE?

look down. He didn't really say look around. Jesus said "Look up!" He said for the disciples to look to Him for the balm, and do it now, not later. Break the huddle and lift up your eyes to Jesus and Jesus only.

CULTIVATE THE SEED FROM THE GREAT SOWER

It is important to remember that the harvesting we speak of concerns the business of spiritual growth, and spiritual growth is about the business of spiritual cultivation. All of us have a seed sown in us by the Great Sower. The question is: will you allow it to germinate? Will you allow it to grow? Will you water it with the Word of God? Will you cultivate it with prayer, knowledge and meditation?

There is a spark of divinity in you, and until you allow it to germinate, there will always be a void in your life. It is there, and it wants to come forth! It is longing after and is hungering for the Word of God. David said, "That as my heart panteth after the water brook so my soul seeketh after Thee." As the swallows fly back to Capistrano, as the homing birds fly home, as the trees lean to the sunshine, so it is with the soul of humankind.

The soul longs for God. There is a seed in all of us that is longing for God. We are called to have our souls be in the harvest. Unchurched people all around us have the seed from the great Sower sown in them as well, and they present the greatest need to be cultivated and harvested. Unchurched people are on our streets, in our neighborhoods, and our jobs. In addition to being harvest for God, won't you be a harvester for Him as well?

> "PRAY YE, THEREFORE, THE LORD OF THE HARVEST, THAT HE WILL SEND FORTH LABORERS INTO HIS HARVEST."

JOIN HIM IN PRAYER

In Matthew 9:35-38, Jesus looked back over Jerusalem with compassion. He saw how weak the people were. They were like sheep without a shepherd. Although I have never done any sheep-herding, I have read about it, and it is my understanding that a sheep without a shepherd is a pitiful thing. Lost sheep will hurt themselves. They will leave the herd and wander off, getting into dangerous situations. Describing the harvest of lost souls to His disciples as sheep without a shepherd, Jesus came to this conclusion: the harvest is bountiful, but the laborers were few to bring it in. "Pray ye, therefore, the Lord of the harvest, that he will send forth laborers into his harvest."

Will you be an answer to Jesus' prayer? Will you respond by joining in prayer with Him today? The need is great and so is the reward. The pay is good, and the wages are present tense. Jesus said everybody will receive the wages, and they all will be glad simultaneously. Oh, those are good wages when everyone is satisfied! Not only are the wages, simultaneously glad wages, satisfying wages for all – they are everlasting wages! In other words, everlasting pay. Don't be guilty of doing too little and being too late. Time is of the essence!

BREAK THE HUDDLE AND ACT TODAY!

In the Gospel of John 4:35, Jesus says, "Do not say I am going to wait four months." In other words, don't procrastinate!" You do not have to wait until April. You do not have to wait until the first of the year. The harvest is ripe now!

BREAK THE
HUDDLE AND
PARTICIPATE
IN THE HARVEST
WHILE YOU
HAVE TIME!

Do you know what happens when you don't pick something when it is ripe? It perishes. Jesus would not have any of his little ones to perish! Don't wait! Don't procrastinate! Don't be guilty of doing too little, and being too late! Don't let the harvest pass you by! Break the huddle and participate in the harvest while you have time!

The good news is that the hard work has already been done! We are privileged to get in on the benefits of work already completed. Break the huddle and start looking for balm in Jesus and in Jesus only. Break the huddle and stop procrastinating! It's time to act! We know not the day or hour when our time to die will come. The person sitting next to you at work might not be there tomorrow. Fanny J. Crosby expressed the sentiment well when she penned the words to, "Pass Me Not, O Gentle Savior":

"Pass me not, O gentle Savior.
Hear my humble cry.
While on others thou art calling.
Do not pass me by."

Have you been putting off until tomorrow what you should be doing today? Have you been looking for balm in all the wrong places while you take your time getting to God's work? You can decide today to break the huddle and participate in the harvest while you have time. Won't you look up to Jesus? Will you be in the harvest, and will you be a harvester for Him? I pray that someone reading this will allow Jesus to begin to cultivate the seed that He's already placed in him or her.

He did the planting. We can help Him with the watering, but God alone will give the increase. As we join in prayer with Jesus, the Lord of the Harvest will send the laborers.

The Bible says if you love God, you'll serve Him. Don't be guilty of having too little response. Don't be guilty of having too little faith, too little initiative, too little acceptance or too little love. Christianity is a "right now" lifestyle. Live today for Him in the fullest way. Break the huddle of complacency and procrastination! Will you do as much as you can, and do it now to harvest souls into the kingdom of God? I pray that you will.

CHAPTER TWELVE
REVIEW QUESTIONS

1. How does the Word of God cut two ways?

2. Revelation 14:14-20 is an illustration of how God's Word cuts two ways. Give a description of each way it cuts in John's vision.

3. Give three biblical examples of people who suffered the consequences of doing too little and being too late.

4. How does the phrase "too little, too late" relate to the urgency of God's harvest?

5. What happened in Jeremiah 8:20-22 that illustrates doing too little and being too late?

6. Fill in the blanks:

(a) The problem is that people are looking for _____ in all the wrong _____ .

(b) The _____, the _____, the _____ is found in Jesus and _____ _____ .

7. Describe what the sickle of mercy, grace and love will harvest at the end.

8. What will the sickle of wrath be used to harvest at the consummation of time?

9. How does our spiritual procrastination lessen the harvest for God's kingdom?

10. Fill in the blanks:

(a) The spark of divinity in every man is _____ after and _____ for the _____ _____ _____ .

(b) The soul _____ for God.

(c) We are called to have _____ _____ be in the harvest.

11. What is the request that Jesus makes to us in Matthew 9:35-38?

FOR DEEPER STUDY

1. Read Revelation 1:1-20 and realize that Jesus was revealing the end of time to John in his vision. What does this mean to you?

2. Read John 10:1-11.ß What does this passage say about the urgency to share Jesus with every person rather than leaving them to look for salvation by other means?

HUDDLE GROUP DISCUSSION

1. How well does the church teach God's Word as a sword that cuts to comfort? Cite a passage that you find particularly helpful in harvesting souls.

2. Is the church effective in teaching God's Word as a sword that cuts to disturb? Cite a passage that convicts the unchurched effectively and brings them into the harvest.

3. Do you think the church needs more or less emphasis on the Book of Revelation to increase the harvest for God's kingdom?

BREAK THE HUDDLE!

In what way are you spiritually procrastinating? Specifically, what do you need to act on? When will you act?

EPILOGUE

Time is Winding Down

> NO ONE KNOWS
> THE DAY OR
> THE HOUR, BUT
> SURELY WE ARE
> IN THE LAST DAYS.

Picture a football game where an electronic digital scoreboard is counting down to zero. Twenty-two players are heavily padded. Eleven are dressed in red uniforms and the eleven others are dressed in gold uniforms. They oppose each other on a chilly autumn day. The band is playing. Pretty girls in short skirts with megaphones are cheering, while four or five men in striped shirts are blowing whistles and taking command. The game is nearly over, and time is winding down. The football teams huddle, preparing for the last play.

Now picture a different kind of scoreboard where the time clock is counting down to zero in the church. People are gathered on a Sunday morning meditating by pipe organ music. Others are clapping and raising their hands in praise to the rhythm of a Hammond organ and keyboard. Men in long robes or dress suits stand high in a center stage position, proclaiming with great fer-

> WE CANNOT
> TARRY, BECAUSE
> TIME IS
> PROMISED
> TO NO ONE.
> IT'S TIME TO BREAK
> THE HUDDLE!

vor messages designed to touch the hearts of the people. The choir is singing and ushers are doing their thing. The church is huddled once again, and time is winding down.

No one knows the day or the hour, but surely we are in the last days. Jesus is coming, and so is Judgement Day. Soon all our works will be tried. If the church is going to beat the clock, we must break the huddle now. We cannot tarry because time is promised to no one. It's time to break the huddle!

During my high school days, we didn't have electronic, digital scoreboards to keep the time or score. We had a table-sized, old-fashioned, long-hand/short-hand Big Ben-type clock, controlled manually by the principals of the schools or their designees. Once when our team was playing in Birmingham, Alabama, we were behind in the score and the time was winding down. Our time-keeper did us a favor by illegally stopping the clock, allowing us to catch up in the score before he let the clock wind down to end the game. The other team was angry and wanted to fight, but we were glad, although we knew we didn't deserve to win.

> ... GOD HAS AN
> ANGEL HOLDING
> BACK THE TIME,
> WAITING FOR
> US TO SCORE.

God's heavenly time clock is also winding down. Likewise, we don't deserve to win, but God has an angel holding back the time, waiting for us to score. We cannot score in the huddle. We cannot score unless we move from our holier-than-thou attitudes and positions. We cannot score until we move from our church lines of scrimmage to God's goal line. We cannot score until we spiritually internalize that the Great Commission is not a divine suggestion. It is a commandment to make disciples. Go, because time is winding down! Break the huddle!

BIBLIOGRAPHY

McCalep, George O. *Faithful Over a Few Things.* Lithonia: Orman Press, 1996.

Crosby, Fanny. "Pass Me Not, O Gentle Savior." P.D.

Unknown (Negro Spiritual), "The Old Ship of Zion." P.D.

Watts, Issac. "We're Marching to Zion." P.D.